D0513574

ARNHEM

OPERATION MARKET GARDEN,
SEPTEMBER 1944

LLOYD CLARK

SUTTON PUBLISHING

First published in 2002 by
Sutton Publishing Limited · Phoenix Mill
Thrupp · Stroud · Gloucestershire · GL5 2BU

British Library Cataloguing in Publication Data
A catalogue record for this book is available from the British Library

ISBN 0-7509-2835-2

Typeset in 12/16pt Sabon.
Typesetting and origination by
Sutton Publishing Limited.
Printed and bound in England by
J.H. Haynes & Co. Ltd. Sparkford.

CONTENTS

For Henry, my mother and father –
John and Pauline Clark – and my brother, Brent.

INTRODUCTION AND ACKNOWLEDGEMENTS

It has been said many times before that British people seem to remember their national military failures as keenly as their military successes. The 1916 Battle of the Somme, for example, is perceived by many as a disaster of gigantic proportions and yet is recalled as readily as Wellington's victory over Napoleon at Waterloo. The continued vigour of the Somme in the collective consciousness of the nation is largely due to the huge casualties that were sustained on just one day, the first day of the battle, when over 57,000 British and Empire troops fell in just a few hours. The reaction of many people to such awful facts is to use words such as 'futile' and wasteful' in an attempt to try and articulate their horror and to believe that 'incompetent donkeys', the High Command, 'unfeelingly' ordered the troops, the 'lions', to their deaths. It is interesting to note, therefore, that in my experience, the mere mention of Operation Market Garden to the initiated leads to hackles being raised and sentiments being proffered which mirror those encountered when battles like the Somme are being discussed. Much of the emotion can, perhaps, be explained by the way in which the British perceive the operation to be (with due apologies to the Americans and the Poles) a 'glorious British failure' and a singular event containing all the ingredients of a great tragedy.

Market Garden was the brainchild of FM Bernard Montgomery who sought to get the stalled British Second Army moving again by dropping a British airborne division deep behind enemy lines to capture 'the prize objective'. The association between Montgomery, a national hero, and the operation is one of its outstanding attractions to Britons. Seen by even his most staunch supporters as one of the darkest stains on his military record, the operation has come to overshadow many (if not all) of Montgomery's European successes. The question of Montgomery's reputation, when combined with the issues surrounding the romance of a bold operation involving ground troops racing against time in order to relieve the beleaguered airborne forces of three nations, goes some way towards explaining why the episode has proved so irresistible to the close attentions of academics, soldiers and the media, and continues to enthral the British public. Millions of words have been written about this remarkable operation and this book is my small contribution to the debate that still surrounds it.

Although I have always found writing to be a largely solitary experience which requires me to live in a bubble of the past that is pricked only occasionally by the needs of a young family, I have also always found that research is a rewarding team effort. While I bear the responsibility for any errors that may occur in this book, I should like to extend my warmest thanks to the 'team' that helped me produce it: Mr Joop van der Linden of Valkenswaard, Holland and Dr Adrian Groeneweg and the staff at the Airborne Forces Museum, Oosterbeek; the staff of the Airborne Forces Museum, Aldershot; the staff of the Central Library, Royal Military Academy Sandhurst (and particularly to Andrew Orgill who has put up with my demands for far too long without due recognition); members of the Department of War Studies, Royal Military Academy Sandhurst; the staff of the Public Record Office, Kew; the staff of the Liddell Hart Military Archives, King's College London; the staff of the Photographic Department and Department of Documents at the Imperial War Museum (IWM); John S. Duvall at the Airborne and Special Operations Museum Foundation(ASOMF); USA; members of the British Commission for Military History, to my publisher Jonathan Falconer and to Ro Horrocks and my battlefield tour friends, including Marion Easton, Gill Willett, Grahame Kingston, Lesley Ratcliffe, Colin and June Meachen and Alan and Janet Lane. I should also like to say a special thank you to the veterans of the operation who, over several years, have done me the honour of answering my numerous questions about those heady days: Mr Donald Shirreff; Mr Len Wright; Sir James Cleminson; Mr Tony Brady; Mr Vivian Taylor and Col Geoffrey Powell. Lastly, however, I must thank my family, Catriona, Freddie, Charlotte and Henry (who was born during the writing of these acknowledgements), who have always put up with my strange hours, frequent trips abroad and scary moods with incredible forbearance. Thanks are also due to my mother, father and brother. Mum and dad unknowingly set me on the road to becoming a professional military historian by taking me to see the film *A Bridge Too Far* several times when I was a boy (and followed it with Cornelius Ryan's book and the film soundtrack for my birthday) and then supported me through my protracted studies years later. Brent, my brother, has also been wonderfully supportive of everything that I have done over the years even though I know that he thinks that what I do for a living is odd.

Lloyd Clark
Royal Military Academy Sandhurst, 2002

ONE

CONCEPTION AND PLANNING

In the weeks after D-Day, 6 June 1944, British, American and Canadian troops began to push out of their Normandy beachhead and strike towards Germany. The Battle of Normandy was a disaster for Hitler, for as the Red Army shattered divisions in the east, resistance to the developing Allied offensives in the west cost Germany nearly half of its 1 million men in theatre and swallowed up resources that were becoming increasingly difficult to replace. Paris was liberated on 25 August and with it came a growing feeling from across the English Channel and the Atlantic Ocean, that the end of the European war was in sight. The news from the fighting front continued to be ebullient over the next couple of weeks and did little to temper the wave of optimism that was washing over the Allies – the German forces had lost their cohesion, were disorganised, demoralised and short of crucial supplies and equipment. The situation did, indeed, look admirable for the supreme commander of the Allied Expeditionary Force, the American general, Dwight Eisenhower, but it belied a number of problems that he needed to sort out with some urgency.

By early September, Gen Omar Bradley's Twelfth Army Group was advancing with Lt Gen Jacob Dever's Sixth Army Group to his south and Gen Bernard Montgomery's Twenty-First Army Group to his north. Good progress was being made, but under Montgomery's command the Canadian First Army, pushing along the North Sea coast, and British Second Army, thrusting into Belgium, were running out of steam. Lt Gen Sir Miles Dempsey had twenty-five infantry divisions and thirteen armoured divisions, a total of 2

XXX Corps's advance through a badly damaged French village during late August 1944. The M4 Sherman tank is armed with a 76-mm gun, two .30-in machine guns and a turret-mounted Browning .50-in M2 Heavy Machine Gun. *(IWM B.9461)*

million men, under his command in Second Army, but as a result of supplies still having to be transported to him from the Normandy beaches, necessaries were running short and, consequently, his tempo was suffering. Second Army had already done what it could to ameliorate these difficulties by stripping down its organisation to the bare essentials, but during the first days of September its spearhead, XXX Corps, progressing at a rate of 50 miles a day, ran

Taken on 1 September 1944, the day of Montgomery's promotion to the rank of field marshal, this photograph shows (from left to right), Lt Gen Henry Crerar, commander of the Canadian First Army; Montgomery and Lt Gen Sir Miles Dempsey, commander of the British Second Army. *(IWM BU.555)*

A meeting of the Chiefs of the Allied Liberation Forces in London on 1 February 1944. From left to right: Gen Omar N. Bradley, Adm Sir Bertram Ramsay, ACM Sir Arthur Tedder, Gen Dwight Eisenhower, Gen Sir Bernard Montgomery, ACM Sir Trafford Leigh Mallory and Maj Gen Walter Bedell Smith. *(IWM CH.12109)*

A conference of American and British general officers held in France in August. From left to right: Lt Gen Courtney H. Hodges, US First Army; Lt Gen Henry Crerar, Canadian First Army; Gen Sir Bernard Montgomery, Twenty-First Army Group; Lt Gen Omar Bradley, US Twelfth Army, and Lt Gen Sir Miles Dempsey, British Second Army. *(IWM B.9473)*

Lt Gen Brian Horrocks, commander of XXX Corps (left), and Lt Gen Sir Miles Dempsey, commander of the British Second Army, at the latter's headquarters on 11 September. Horrocks was still suffering from the wounds that he had received in Italy in 1943 and was not a well man during Operation Market Garden. *(IWM BU.876)*

into real logistical difficulties. Thus, having taken Brussels on 3 September and Antwerp on the following day, Second Army were forced to suspend their advance.

Meanwhile, while Dempsey spent time examining his lines of communication as well as the enemy to his front, Montgomery was busy planning the next phase of his logistically troubled offensive. The fruit of his labour was the profoundly ambitious Operation Comet in which Second Army would be thrown into the gap which had emerged between the Fifteenth and Seventh Armies and, aided by a division of British and a brigade of Polish airborne troops, cross the Lower Rhine at Arnhem. Comet was something of a challenge to the 'broad front' strategy that Eisenhower had been pursuing, for although it did not preclude the supreme commander's ambition to attack Germany from both sides of the Ardennes, Comet would require its exponents to have preferential logistical provision and Eisenhower was keen to ensure that no one commander was given the opportunity to try and win the war in Europe on his own. Nevertheless, Montgomery, promoted to the rank of field marshal on 1 September, was not afraid of a confrontation with his superior, for he thought that his arguments for a concentrated thrust, a 'narrow front', would be beneficial strategically, for it would provide a platform from which to launch an attack on Germany's industrial heartland, the Ruhr. As for the logistics that would be required for Comet to succeed, Montgomery was clear, the broad front dispersed and

An interesting study of a controversial man. This picture of Gen Sir Bernard Montgomery, commander of the British Twenty-First Army Group, was taken in France as he briefed Allied war correspondents shortly after the Normandy landings. (IWM B.5337)

Once liberated, the people of Antwerp rounded up German prisoners and Belgian collaborators and held them in a lion's cage at the local zoo.
(IWM BU.561)

therefore exacerbated the Allied supply problems, while channelling supplies to a prioritised Twenty-First Army Group would ease the burden on the supply chain as it was the closest Army Group to the Normandy beaches. A telegram sent by Montgomery to Eisenhower on 4 September outlined his arguments:

. . . (1) I consider we have now reached a stage where one really powerful and full blooded thrust towards Berlin is likely to get there and thus end the German war. (2) We have not enough maintenance resources for two full blooded thrusts. (3) The selected thrust must have all the maintenance resources it needs without qualification and any other operation must do the best it can with what is left over. (4) There are only two possible thrusts one via the Ruhr and the other via Metz and the Saar. (5) In my opinion the thrust likely to give the best and quickest results is the northern one via the Ruhr . . .

The wording and tone of this communication, however, did little more than play to Eisenhower's fear that Montgomery wished to strike out alone. The supreme commander therefore replied on 5 September:

I do not agree that it should be initiated at this moment to the exclusion of all other maneuvers . . . No re-allocation of our present resources would be adequate to sustain a thrust on Berlin . . . Accordingly, my intention is initially to occupy the Saar and the Ruhr, and by the time we have done this, Havre and Antwerp should be available to maintain one or both of the thrusts you mention . . . I have always given, and still give, priority to the Ruhr and the northern route of advance . . .

Maj Gen Alan Adair, commander of the Guards Armoured Division, salutes the cheering crowds in Brussels as the city is liberated. *(IWM BU.480A)*

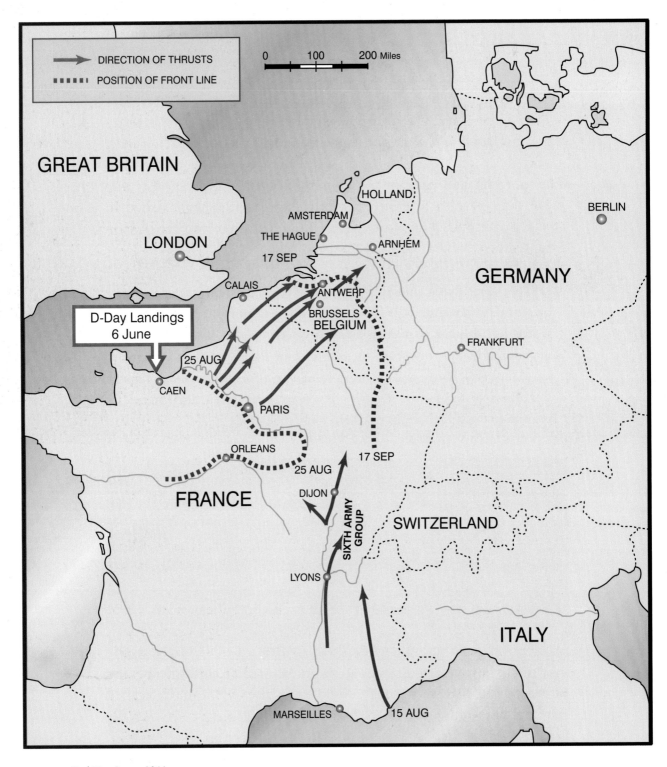

North-West Europe, 1944.

Montgomery visiting the Albert canal area on 15 September where he met some of his troops and discussed details of the coming Operation Garden with his armoured commanders. From left to right: Maj Gen A.H.S. Adair, commander of the Guards Armoured Division; Montgomery; Lt Gen B.G. Horrocks, commander of XXX Corps; and Maj Gen G.P.B. Roberts, commander of 11th Armoured Division. *(IWM B.9973)*

This disagreement, made all the more intense due to their clashing personalities, continued for several days and in that time Eisenhower remained unconvinced.

Meanwhile, while the debate about future strategy was in full flow, Second Army endeavoured to husband enough resources to continue its advance. In such circumstances it seems inconceivable that discussions about strategy were not centred around the opening of the port of Antwerp which could have provided a much needed forward harbour, but neither Eisenhower nor Montgomery were in favour of this as they wished to reapply pressure on the retreating Germans as soon as possible, and clearing the 60 miles of Scheldt estuary of enemy troops and mines would, they believed, take months. However, the decision to dismiss the port as an immediate objective did have an unfortunate corollary effect, for when

The village of Hetchel in Belgium on 12 September soon after it had been cleared of German troops. This village was on the main supply route to the Meuse-Escaut canal which had already been crossed by the Guards Armoured Division. *(IWM B.10036)*

As the British advanced towards the Meuse-Escaut canal it became clear that the Germans were recovering their poise. Here German prisoners carry a wounded man on a stretcher while British troops move into the front line. *(IWM B.10031)*

combined with the increasing British focus upon a Rhine crossing, it led eyes to stray from the opportunity that had been presented to Lt Gen Sir Brian Horrock's XXX Corps to advance a further 15 miles and block the escape route of the Fifteenth Army which was otherwise trapped in the Scheldt estuary. The escape of Gen Gustave von Zangen's men and equipment was an important oversight in the fog of war that was to have a great impact on events in Holland during the weeks that followed.

When XXX Corps did move forward again on 6 September, it was towards the Albert canal as a preliminary to Operation Comet. Leading the attack were Gen Alan Adair's Guards Armoured Division, which probed forward towards the Belgian border with Holland some 40 miles east of Antwerp. As they did so it became immediately clear that German resistance was increasing, so much so that it was not until 10 September that the Irish Guards seized intact the de Groot bridge over the Meuse-Escaut canal near Neerpelt on the road that led to Eindhoven and then on to Nijmegen and Arnhem – the bridge that was to become known as 'Joe's bridge' in honour of the commander of the Irish Guards Group, Lt Col J.O.E. Vandeleur. The revitalised enemy had fatal consequences for Operation Comet, for it convinced Montgomery that he needed to dig deeper into the resources of the newly formed First Allied Airborne Army (FAAA), the strategic reserve that Eisenhower had made available to him, and to reassess his resource requirements. Montgomery's new plan was called Operation Market Garden.

Montgomery pitched the Market Garden plan to Eisenhower at a meeting between the two men in Brussels on 10 September. The idea was that the FAAA would seize numerous river crossings, including one over the Lower Rhine at Arnhem, ahead of an advancing XXX Corps which would then push on to the Ijesselmeer and trap German forces in western Holland. From this position, Montgomery argued, it would be possible to attack towards the Ruhr (in operations coordinated with the United States forces), isolate the area, and then, if the opportunity arose, advance to Berlin. The plan was bold, ambitious and not a little seductive to Eisenhower, who immediately saw merits in what was being proposed. Although

Gen George Patton (left), Gen Omar Bradley (centre) and Gen Sir Bernard Montgomery share a joke on 7 July 1944 in France. Montgomery had just presented the ribbon of British decorations to a number of American officers and men for bravery and devotion to duty in the Normandy fighting. *(IWM B.6551)*

Market Garden was clearly in line with Montgomery's desire for a narrow front, Eisenhower believed that if carefully handled the operation could be incorporated into his strategy, for it sought to provide a crucial Rhine crossing point. As a result Eisenhower accepted the scheme, but would not be drawn at the meeting to discuss what would happen after the immediate objectives of the operation had been secured or Montgomery's demands for supply supremacy.

In order to ascertain exactly what Eisenhower had agreed to, Montgomery signalled his boss on the 11 September saying he could not envisage Market Garden being launched until 23 September for want of adequate supplies. A reply came back from Eisenhower in the person of his Chief-of-Staff, Lt Gen Walter Bedell Smith, who visited Montgomery on 12 September to clear up the matter. Bedell Smith said that the British Second Army would receive the supplies that it required to cross the Rhine and that the US Third Army, commanded by Lt Gen George Patton, would be temporarily halted while resources from Bradley's Twelfth Army Group were transferred to the US First Army on Twenty-First Army Group's right flank. What this amounted to was supply priority for Montgomery until 1 October in order for Market Garden to be carried out – but nothing more. Nevertheless, whether in denial or confident that Eisenhower was caving in, Montgomery wrote to the Vice Chief of the Imperial General Staff, Sir Archibald Nye, on 12 September, '[Eisenhower] has given way . . . So we have gained a great victory. I feel somewhat overcome by it all but hope we shall now win the war reasonably quickly'. In reality Eisenhower had not 'given way', he had merely agreed to an operation that was a welcome thrust within his own broad front concept. This truth slowly dawned on Montgomery over the days that followed, but planning had already started, and having listened to Bedell Smith's assurances, he set the launch date for 17 September.

There were two elements to Operation Market Garden: the airborne plan, Operation Market, and the ground plan, Operation Garden. In

Garden the British Second Army, led by XXX Corps and spearheaded by the Guards Armoured Division, were to advance from Joe's bridge near Neerpelt and advance through Eindhoven on the afternoon of the first day, Nijmegen, during the evening of the second day, to Arnhem which, according to Horrocks, could be reached by the afternoon of the third day. There were, however, many potential obstacles to success, for there were many ways in which the enemy could slow or even halt the progress of the XXX Corps. These problems largely stemmed from the fact that the advance would have to be up a single narrow road. This road was raised in certain places and, to the advantage of the defending Germans, was often bordered by woods and crossed many waterways. As a result, it was essential that these bridges were not destroyed by the enemy if XXX Corps were to reach their objectives in good time, that the road was not cut by the enemy, and that the towns and villages along the route did not become choke points. Part of the plan to ensure that XXX Corps were not delayed or stopped as they advanced was the protection afforded to its flanks from XII Corps, advancing on the left, and VIII Corps (which initially would consist of just one division) advancing on the right. However, as it was likely that the flank protection might get bogged down as it engaged the enemy, it was crucial that air power was available to the ground troops. Close air support and battlefield air interdiction were possible as the Allies possessed both the resources and air superiority required to provide them, but there were obstacles to their delivery due to the density of air traffic caused by the insertion and resupply of the airborne troops of the FAAA who were to aid the ground advance by seizing bridges and key terrain prior to the arrival of XXX Corps.

The FAAA was a new organisation formed on 8 August and commanded by Lt Gen Lewis Brereton. The formation consisted of the US XVIII Airborne Corps, comprised of the 17th, 82nd and 101st US Airborne Divisions under Maj Gen Matthew Ridgeway, and the 1st British Airborne Corps, commanded by Brereton's deputy, Lt Gen Frederick Browning, consisting of the 1st and 6th British Airborne Divisions, the 1st Independent Polish Brigade and the air-transportable 52nd (Lowland) Division. This army, one-sixth of Eisenhower's fighting strength, was keen to justify its existence

The commander of the First Allied Airborne Army, Lt Gen Lewis Brereton, during a visit to British 6th Airborne Division in March 1944. Formerly commander of the US Ninth Air Force, his headquarters were at Sunninghill Park near Ascot. *(IWM H.40769)*

after sixteen previous operations had been cancelled during its short existence, and the US Chief of Staff, Gen George Marshal, and the Commanding General Army Air Forces, Gen Henry Arnold, were keen to see what a large-scale airborne attack deep in enemy territory could accomplish. Montgomery's plan was, therefore, the right operation at the right time, and almost as soon as Market Garden was announced it began to attain a decidedly unstoppable momentum.

Operation Market was intended for the 101st Airborne Division, commanded by Maj Gen Maxwell Taylor, to take the bridges between Eindhoven and Veghel; Brig Gen (promoted to Major General during the battle) James Gavin's 82nd Airborne Division was to seize the bridges from Grave to Nijmegen; and Maj Gen Roy Urquhart's 1st Airborne Division, with the attached 1st Independent Polish Brigade, commanded by Maj Gen Stanislaw Sosabowski, was to capture the bridges over the Lower Rhine at Arnhem. All three airborne divisions were also expected to take vital ground, especially the 82nd Airborne Division which was to command the Groesbeek Heights overlooking Nijmegen and bordering the Reichswald, in order to protect their bridges and keep the single road open for the advance of XXX Corps to Arnhem. The question as to why Arnhem was chosen by Montgomery as the place to cross the Rhine is an interesting one, especially in light of what Browning is often quoted as having said at the final planning conference with Montgomery on 10 September: 'I think that we might be going a bridge too far.' Leaving aside the fact that Browning saw Dempsey on that day and not Montgomery, the remark was an unlikely one for Browning to have made as he had been a great proponent of Operation Comet, an operation that sought to achieve something very similar to Market Garden, but with far fewer airborne troops. Moreover, Browning was aware of the advantages that an Arnhem crossing provided: an opportunity for the British to outflank the most northerly defences of the Siegfried Line and, unlike a crossing further south at Wesel, for Allied transportation aircraft to side-step German flak and fighter defences protecting the Ruhr. A crossing at Arnhem also had the important benefit of allowing the more rapid

Maj Gen Frederick 'Boy' Browning in October 1942, aged forty-five, when commanding 1st British Airborne Division. He was married to the famous novelist, Daphne du Maurier, and was a qualified glider pilot who had won the DSO in the First World War while with the Grenadier Guards. By September 1944 Browning was commander of I British Airborne Corps and deputy commander of the First Allied Airborne Army. (IWM H.24128)

Maj Gen 'Roy' Urquhart, commander of the British 1st Airborne Division. The 43-year-old Urquhart took command of the division in January 1944 after the previous GOC, Maj Gen G.F. Hopkinson, had been killed in Italy. (IWM H.40947)

Maj Gen Maxwell D. Taylor, commander of the US 101st Airborne Division, salutes from the door of his C-47 prior to taking off for Holland on 17 September. Taylor had commanded the division in Normandy and before that had led the division's artillery in Sicily and Italy. *(ASOMF)*

Gen Montgomery presenting the DSO to Maj Gen Maxwell D. Taylor, commander of the US 101st Airborne Division, for gallantry in action at Carentan, Normandy, on 12 June 1944. *(IWM B.6543)*

Opposite: Brig Gen James Gavin, commander of the US 82nd Airborne Division, makes some final adjustments to his equipment before emplaning on 17 September. Gavin was an intelligent, quiet ex-ranker who, at thirty-seven, was the youngest divisional commander in the US Army. *(ASOMF)*

clearance of the German V2 rocket bases on the Dutch coast, which Winston Churchill, the British Prime Minister, wanted dealt with as a matter of priority, as these missiles had recently begun to slam into England. The reason why it was the British airborne divisions that were given the task of dropping 64 miles behind enemy lines at Arnhem can be found in a variety of facts: Market Garden was a British scheme, Montgomery's plan put into action by Browning; it was the 'Arnhem Division' that was most likely to be stranded as XXX Corps struggled forward, and although those troops dropped at Arnhem would be the most vulnerable troops, they would also receive the lion's share of the glory if the operation was a success.

The British airborne division were certainly ready for the challenge, for its component parts had not seen action since 1943 and had recently suffered a raft of cancelled operations. Trying to keep these highly trained and motivated troops occupied and out of trouble was not easy for their officers. Maj Geoffrey Powell, a company commander in 156th Parachute Battalion, commented in his excellent memoirs *Men At Arnhem*:

> It was understandable that nerves had frayed and discipline had upset during the summer. More and more men had drifted away, absent without leave, to return when boredom set in or consciences started to bite. Fights outside pubs with GIs from nearby American units became a regular Saturday night fixture . . . After the hysteria of the capture of Paris, the British and American armies were still sweeping on towards the German frontier, virtually unopposed. The war could well be over before we got into it. 'The Stillborn Division', we had started to call ourselves, to be kept for use in the victory parade, nice and tidy in our smart, red berets.

Browning was ready and willing to send these men into action, for although he was more aware than most of the perils involved in airborne operations, he also understood the enormity of the prize if Market Garden succeeded. Confident in the professionalism of his troops, he thought the operation a chance worth taking. On the evening of 10 September Browning briefed his commanders at his

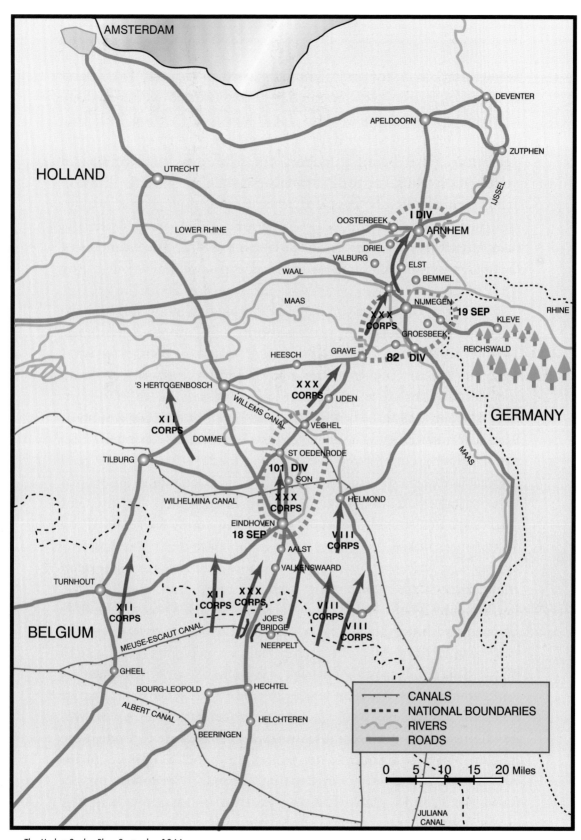

The Market Garden Plan, September 1944.

headquarters in Ascot and planning started in earnest. The largest airborne operation ever mounted, Market Garden was incredibly complex with great opportunity for things to go wrong. It is true that there were just seven days between Eisenhower agreeing to the operation and it being launched, but while this time frame did undoubtedly cause serious difficulties when it came to decision making, this had to be expected when employing airborne warfare and, it must be remembered, Operation Comet did provide the planners with a firm platform from which to work. The essentials of the plan were quickly dealt with; the details were filled in as the week progressed.

The airborne lifts were to take place during daylight hours as a 'no moon' period precluded the usual airborne night drops and landings. The problem with this was that the enemy could, of course, see what was going on and enemy fighter aircraft and flak batteries could do considerable damage to the vulnerable, slow-moving air transport. This problem was to be ameliorated, however, by the application of Allied air superiority in a comprehensive preliminary bombing raid and a fighter escort for the massive air armada. It would have been preferable to have transported all of the airborne troops in one lift so as to take best advantage of their primary asset, surprise, but there were not enough transport aircraft for more than half of the 35,000-man force to be inserted on the first day. Pressure was applied by Brereton on Maj Gen Paul Williams, the American commander of the air transport plan, for more than one lift a day, but Williams would not agree as he said that his aircrew would be fatigued and his ground crews would need to repair the anticipated battle damage and carry out aircraft maintenance. This reluctance to be flexible and to take a risk in such an operation seems unreasonable, but Williams had been told to expect 40 per cent air losses on the first day and it is perhaps understandable that he was unwilling to put his precious aircrews and aircraft in even more danger than was absolutely necessary. The knock-on effects of his decision were, however, far-reaching and had a dramatic impact upon the ground plan. The aggravation of multiple lifts, for example, immediately demanded that the airborne commanders had

1st Airborne Division at Haceby before Operation Market Garden. Montgomery is talking to the commander of 1st Parachute Brigade, Brig G.W. Lathbury, and behind them are the divisional commander, Maj Gen R.E. Urquhart, and Lord Brownlow. *(IWM H.36657)*

to prioritise the arrival of their resources, especially after it had been decided that size of the lifts were to be different for each division, with the 101st Airborne Division receiving the largest share, the 82nd Airborne Division the next biggest, and the 1st Division receiving the smallest. Although the aim of the plan was to get XXX Corps across the Lower Rhine at Arnhem, the planners decided that they were unlikely to get that far unless the airborne divisions further to the south had adequate resources to take and hold their objectives. Thus, the British and Polish airborne troops were planned to arrive in three lifts spread over three days with the smallest being the first-day lift. As a result Urquhart decided to take just six infantry battalions on the 17th with a higher percentage of his supporting arms, while his field artillery were to arrive on the 18th. Both American airborne divisions decided to drop all nine of

Brig Gen James Gavin, commander of the US 101st Airborne Division, briefs his staff on 16 September, the day before Operation Market Garden was launched. Gavin had previously led 505th Parachute Infantry Regiment in Sicily and Italy. *(ASOMF)*

their parachute battalions on the first day with the 101st in a position where they could take more more supporting arms than the 82nd. Whether the plan should have been 'bottom to top' as it was or, with the British airborne division clearly the most vulnerable, as they were least likely to benefit from the initial surprise of the operation and a speedy union with XXX Corps, planners should have provided for a 'top to bottom' operation, remains a moot point, but what is clear is that Browning unnecessarily exacerbated the transportation difficulties by commandeering thirty-six valuable gliders in the first lift to deliver his headquarters into Gavin's sector. Browning was keen to lead the airborne troops into battle and aimed to direct operations through his British Airborne Corps until each airborne division came under the command of XXX Corps when they achieved union, but such an admirable gesture was an inefficient use of resources and an unaffordable luxury in the circumstances.

Once the airborne troops were on the ground, the impact of multiple lifts did not suddenly disappear, in fact they became even more tangible. With one lift a complete airborne division could be used to strike out towards its objectives within an hour or so of landing if their surprise was sufficient enough to have dislocated the enemy. With a series of lifts, however, a proportion of the first lift troops would have to be deployed to defend the drops zones (DZs) for the parachutists and landing zones (LZs) for the gliders for subsequent lifts, thus diluting the division's initial attacking force. It was therefore vital that the chosen DZs and LZs were as close as possible to the objectives so that the diminished and lightly armed attacking troops, the vast majority of whom would be on foot, had as good a chance as possible of attaining them. Nevertheless, when choosing the DZs and LZs, planners had not only to take into consideration their proximity to the objectives but also numerous other factors including the suitability of the terrain and the position of enemy anti-aircraft defences. Thus, the situation of the DZs and LZs for Market Garden was a compromise in virtually all cases, and none more so than for the 1st Airborne Division. For the insertion of Urquhart's men, the planners could not find any suitable ground close to their objectives due to the number of anti-aircraft guns in the vicinity, which, even with a preliminary aerial bombardment on such positions, posed a threat. Furthermore, the landing of gliders and parachutists at the northern end of the bridge was not possible because of the density of the buildings and the ground was too wet for glider landings at the southern end. In fact, the delivery of any airborne troops close to Arnhem bridge was highly problematical, because once aircraft had disgorged their cargoes, the transportation aircraft or tugs would have had to over-fly Deelen airfield, 7 miles to the north of Arnhem, and its potentially murderous flak. With Williams already having made it clear that he could hardly afford to lose a single aircraft, this was not an idea which was pursued. It is true that the Polish Brigade were planned to land on the south side of Arnhem bridge on the third day, but this was because all of the German anti-air defences in the area were to have been neutralised by that stage. In the circumstances, therefore, the only possible DZs and LZs were to be found in the countryside to the west of Arnhem. Here, fortunately, was ground perfectly suited to airborne needs in terms of the nature of the ground and its size, but the designated areas were between 4 and 9 miles from the division's objectives. Urquhart was well aware of the difficulties that such distances presented to his mission, but he had little choice in the matter and so did what he could to take the main bridge as quickly as possible. He therefore demanded that his 1st Parachute Brigade moved quickly to their objectives and also planned to despatch Maj Freddie Gough's jeep transported Reconnaissance Squadron the 7 miles into Arnhem as a *coup de main* force to seize the bridge and there to await the arrival of the other units. The nightmare scenario was, however, that the enemy would be capable of quickly setting up defensive positions between Arnhem and the DZs and LZs, thus preventing the attacking airborne forces from reaching the bridge.

During the two weeks that passed between the Allied capture of Brussels and the launching of Market Garden, the Germans greatly increased their ability to defend against such an attack. FM Walter Model, the capable commander of German Army Group B, had the unenviable task of halting Twenty-First Army Group's advance and

Generalfeldmarschall Walter Model, commander of German Army Group B, had the unenviable task of halting the advance of Montgomery's Twenty-First Army Group in September 1944. Model was having lunch at his headquarters in Oosterbeek when British airborne troops began to land just a few miles to the west, but his response to the attack was swift and assured. *(IWM MH.12850)*

quickly turning the disorganised mass of German troops that had pulled back from the Seine into something that resembled a fighting force. To this end Gen Kurt Student, commander of the hastily formed First Parachute Army, was despatched to the Belgian–Dutch border to stem the haemorrhaging of disorientated German troops into the Dutch interior. While the retreat was at its height on 5 September, Student was at his headquarters 15 miles north-west of Eindhoven at Vught determinedly doing what he could to strengthen German defences while awaiting the arrival of his troops: 6 parachute regiments, 2 convalescent regiments and 10,000 Luftwaffe personnel. By this stage in the war, few German units were of a strength to warrant their denomination and often contained troops of very mixed quality, but Student made good use of the scant resources that were available. By 6 September the 719th Division were digging in north of Antwerp and a defensive line was being established on the Albert canal by the first of Student's own parachute troops to arrive and Gen Kurt Chill's Kampfgruppe, a balanced fighting unit that contained the shattered remains of his 85th Division and the remnants of two others. It was Kampfgruppe Chill that the Guards Armoured Division ran into as they probed forward, first towards the Albert canal and then in their struggle to establish their bridgehead over the Meuse-Escaut canal. This experience told the British that the

Germans were rapidly recovering some of their strength, and indeed, by 8 September they had plugged the majority of the holes in their line from Antwerp to Maastricht, helped by the arrival of Student's parachute regiments which were divided between Kampfgruppe Walther and Kampfgruppe Erdmann. Behind the 40,000 men that constituted the German First Parachute Army by 17 September, was the escaped Fifteenth Army that amounted to over 65,0000 men and 225 guns by the same date. To their east and moving from Germany towards Holland, were the 107th Panzer Brigade and Corps Feldt that contained a little armour and a mixture of training, administrative and Luftwaffe troops. Already in Holland, however, and taking up a position behind the Fifteenth Army beyond the Maas, were troops commanded by Gen Friedrich Christiansen's Armed Forces Command Netherlands. These men were yet another amalgam of different units from all parts of the armed forces and from these Kampfgruppe von Tettau was produced. Newly arrived on 7 September was also the remnants of II SS Panzer Corps, commanded by SS Gen Willi Bittrich. This Corps consisted of the 9th and 10th SS Panzer Divisions commanded by Lt Col Walther Harzer and Col

Generaloberst Kurt Student, commander of the First Parachute Army that was ordered to plug the Antwerp-Maastricht gap in early September 1944. Student had been central to the development of German airborne forces, but had not held operational command since the losses suffered during the taking of Crete in 1941. *(IWM MH.6100)*

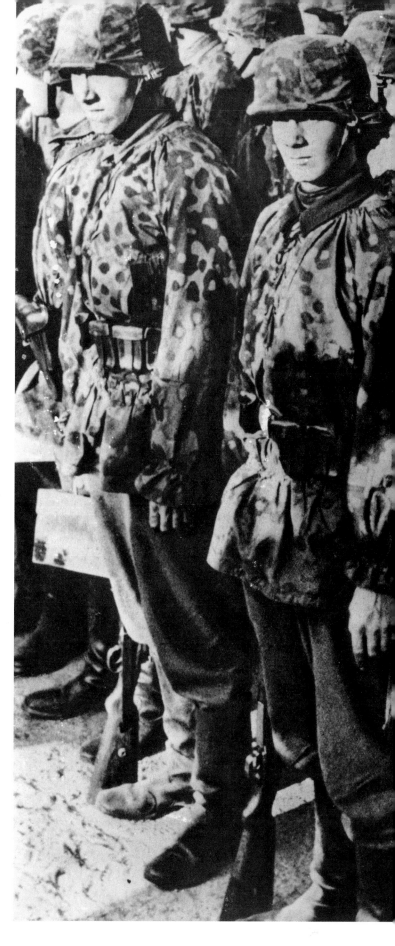

Left: German prisoners taken by the British as they liberated Belgium in early September. Many believed at this time that the Germans were on the verge of collapse and that the war would soon be over. *(IWM B.10030)*

Right: Soldiers of the Waffen-SS in summer pattern camouflage smocks. They are armed with KAR-98K 7.9-mm rifles with ammunition pouches carried around their waists. *(IWM MH.226)*

Heinz Harmel respectively. Although relatively weak, equalling the strength of only a weak brigade of about 6,500 men with a handful of tanks, some artillery and Self Propelled (SP) guns, both contained experienced soldiers of some considerable quality and both divisions had been trained to defend against an airborne attack when they had been in Normandy. The presence of these troops near Arnhem, together with those others that had been rapidly collated, reorganised and thrown into a hastily developed defensive position, clearly reveals the way in which the Germans had, by mid-September, managed to create order out of chaos – but what did the Allies know of the enemy situation?

The amount of Allied intelligence being processed at various headquarters during the early autumn of 1944 was immense. The Allied onslaught had led to the availability of an overwhelming amount of information which had to be collated, categorised, written up, distributed and then acted upon before it went stale. In such circumstances it was extremely difficult to separate the important from the non-important, the accurate from the inaccurate, but

The Guards Armoured Division on the Dutch border immediately before the launch of Operation Market Garden. It was through this type of countryside that the British Second Army had to advance as they pushed north towards Arnhem. *(IWM B.10033)*

the general tone of the intelligence was positive, optimistic even. With the Germans 'on the run' as the Allied front line closed in on Germany, there was an irresistible feeling within the Allied camp that victory was in sight. High morale is indispensable to any army, but it can also lead to the hazards of complacency, and a degree of smugness and self-congratulation was beginning to pervade

Eisenhower's forces. To this end, although it was true that the German forces in Holland were disorganised, demoralised, tired and of low quality when the intelligence for Operation Comet was collected, this was not quite the case, as was seen, by 17 September. Nevertheless, the Allied assumption was that any advantage that the Germans had been able to wrestle from the hiatus enforced on Twenty-First Army Group by their logistical difficulties, would be over-ridden by the paralysis to be created by Market Garden's increased airborne punch. Some Allied soldiers, however, remained unconvinced. Sosabowski, for example, the commander of the Polish Brigade, thought that Browning was being overly and unduly disparaging of the Germans, while Maj Brian Urquhart (who was not related to the commander of the British airborne division), the senior intelligence officer at Airborne Corps headquarters, became increasingly concerned at the information that was being passed on to him about enemy movements. From various sources both Brian Urquhart and Browning knew of the existence of II SS Panzer Corps in the Arnhem area and personnel at FAAA headquarters and above were in possession of more detailed information obtained from Ultra. The Ultra decrypts of German Enigma codes had allowed the Allies to follow the withdrawal of enemy troops into Holland and gave them considerable knowledge about important units, the whereabouts and strength of the 9th and 10th SS Panzer Divisions, for example. Browning, privy to diluted Ultra information, passed down what he knew to his subordinate commanders on 11 September so that they

could make their plans, and this included news that German armour was in the Arnhem vicinity. Roy Urquhart said in his memoirs, 'Browning himself told me that we were not likely to encounter anything more than a brigade group supported by a few tanks'. This was accurate information, and so it seems that if there was an intelligence problem it was that when the information percolated down to the field commanders at the sharp end, it lacked the valuable detail that they so desperately required. The most detailed intelligence summary that 1st Airborne Division received in the run up to Market Garden came from Browning on 13 September :

> The enemy is fighting determinedly along the line ALBERT and ESCAUT canals and from ANTWERP to inclusive MAASTRICHT. His line is held by remnants of some good divisions, including Parachute Divisions, and by some new arrivals from HOLLAND. They are fighting well but have few reserves. The total armoured strength is probably not more than 50-100 tanks, mostly Mark IV. There is every sign of the enemy strengthening the river and canal lines through NIJMEGEN and ARNHEM, especially flak, but the troops manning them are not numerous and many are of a low category. The flak is sited for dual purpose – both AA and ground.

What is important to note is that despite the intelligence that the Allies possessed at the higher levels, nobody thought that the operation should be cancelled. Quite simply, there was a great deal of pressure for the operation to go ahead and there was a good deal of confidence, possibly misplaced, that the Germans would be unable to resist against such a thrust. Operation Market Garden seems to have quickly assumed a sacrosanct position among Allied designs, wonderful if it succeeded, not fatal if it failed, but interesting and intuitive whatever happened. In such circumstances what Roy Urquhart later wrote of his airborne division was also true of Montgomery, Browning and many of those men that enabled Market Garden to rise off the planning table and into occupied Holland: 'We approached the state of mind when we weren't thinking as hard about the risks as we possibly had done earlier.'

TWO

17 SEPTEMBER – THE ASSAULT

The first rumbles of thunder that announced the coming Allied storm were heard in occupied Holland the night before Operation Market Garden began. As the airborne troops that were soon to be plucked from the country of their birth and transported to continental Europe were receiving their final briefings and checking their equipment, Allied fighters and bombers were taking off on missions that sought to disorientate the enemy and destroy their troublesome flak batteries, airfields and barracks. This preparation was deemed essential if as many of the airborne troops as possible were to arrive on Dutch soil safely and accurately and their precious air transport returned to England in readiness for the second lift. The attacking Lancasters, Mosquitoes and B-17 Flying Fortresses did their work thoroughly that night, for during the first lift the Germans found it difficult to launch their fighter aircraft in order to antagonise the Allied aerial convoy, and the guns of the German flak batteries, many of which were hit more than once, were unable to project their destruction into the skies. The following morning, as the Germans assessed the damage caused by these Allied raids and made their reports to their superiors, British and American airborne troops of three Allied airborne divisions made their final preparations at twenty-two airfields in southern and eastern England. The two American airborne divisions had both jumped into action in Normandy early on D-Day, but their casualties had been heavy, and so for the replacements that had recently joined them in England, the surge of adrenaline that preceded embarkation on to the transport aircraft was entirely new. The British airborne

division had not fought together before, but it too was comprised of a mixture of battle-hardened veterans and enthusiastic novices. As these two groups of soldiers basked in the morning sun waiting to enplane, their thoughts might well have reflected their relative experience, but they were united by the relief that it looked as though the waiting was over and the division was, at last, going into battle.

By late morning the sky was filled with over 3,000 aircraft and the throbbing of their engines brought people of south-eastern England out into their gardens and into the streets to see what was happening. What they saw when they looked skyward on that Battle of Britain Day, few would ever forget, for the 5-mile wide columns of aircraft took an hour to pass their towns and villages as they flew steadily towards the English Channel and projected an image of such great Allied military power that the inevitable conclusion of the onlookers was that the war, surely, could not last much longer. Of the 1,534 Dakota, Albemarle, Stirling and Halifax aircraft that took off on 17 September, 491 towed Horsa, Hamilcar or Waco gliders,

Ground and aircrew of a Mark IV Short Stirling from 620 Squadron at RAF Fairford during the summer of 1944. *(J. Falconer)*

Left: Twin lines of C-47 Dakotas full of their precious airborne cargo, prepare for take off from an airfield in England on 17 September. *(ASOMF)*

Lt Gen Lewis Brereton (right) talks to Col Howard 'Skeets' Johnson, commanding officer of the 501st Parachute Infantry Regiment, US 101st Airborne Division, prior to his drop in Holland on 17 September. *(ASOMF)*

and 1,000 P-51 Mustangs, P-38 Lightnings, Spitfires, Tempests and Mosquitoes provided a fighter escort. Their journeys on two routes over the North Sea and Belgium to the DZs and LZs in Holland were uneventful, with just a very few aircraft having to return to England due to technical difficulties and, thankfully for the men trapped inside their fragile transport, there was very little action from either German fighter aircraft or flak batteries. The men of XXX Corps in Belgium also looked skyward that Sunday as the

Men of the US 101st Airborne Division waiting to board a CG-4A glider on 17 September. Its tug, a C-47 Dakota, can be seen in the background. Many of the glider passengers took time to decorate their transportation with chalk pictures and messages. Bearing in mind the vulnerabilities of the flimsy gliders that landed their occupants behind enemy lines with very limited equipment and firepower, it seems that a sense of humour was essential for all airlanding soldiers. *(ASOMF)*

A slightly detached Lt Gen Frederick 'Boy' Browning, commander of the 1st British Airborne Corps, looks on as ACM Sir Arthur Tedder, deputy supreme commander of the Allied Expeditionary Force, discusses plans with an American brigadier-general on the morning of 17 September at RAF Harwell. *(IWM CH.13856)*

aircraft containing the men of the 101st Airborne Division flew over their positions and were no less impressed than the civilians in England had been just an hour or so before. But unlike their brethren on the home front, they faced the immediate prospect of breaking out of their bridgehead in an attempt to forge a link with these highly trained warriors. The Germans, on the other hand, viewed the sight of the aerial armada with a feeling of impending doom, for they understood that it was a clear sign that an Allied storm was about to break.

The charismatic Horrocks had outlined the Market Garden plan to his senior commanders in a cinema in Bourg Leopold on Saturday 16 September. When he came to the details of Operation Garden, he emphasised the need for XXX Corps to advance with speed up the

A wonderful group photograph of Parachute Regiment troops at their airfield on the morning of 17 September just minutes before they donned their equipment and boarded their C-47 for Holland. The man standing on the right is a lieutenant and at the opposite end of the line up crouching is a soldier of the Royal Army Service Corps. (IWM K.7590)

British airborne troops enjoying the sun at RAF Harwell in Oxfordshire – the home of 295 and 570 Squadrons – on the morning of 17 September. Behind them are a number of Horsa gliders with various messages to the Germans written in chalk on their fuselages. It is likely that these men are either from the 1st Airlanding Light Regiment RA, or from the HQ 1st Airborne Corps who were to land in the Groesbeek Heights near Nijmegen. (IWM CH.13859)

Men of the US 82nd Airborne Division emplane on the morning of 17 September. American parachutists carried a reserve parachute strapped to their chests (unlike their British counter-parts) but they would have been of little use had the main parachute failed, as they were in the air for just a few seconds. (IWM EA.37734)

Top: Airborne soldiers wave farewell to a Horsa glider taking off from RAF Harwell on 17 September. It is possible that these troops were waiting to be transported to Holland as part of the second lift on the following day. *(J. Falconer)*

Opposite, top: Parachutists of the US 101st Airborne Division prepare to board their Douglas C-47 Dakota on 17 September. The division was to suffer some 2,118 casualties during Operation Market Garden. *(IWM EA.37750)*

Opposite, bottom: A brew, served by a US Staff Sergeant cook, for Parachute Regiment soldiers on the morning of 17 September. A captain, with map case attached to his smock and bacon sandwich firmly clasped in his hand, enjoys what he knows might be his last meal on English soil for some considerable time. *(IWM K.7589)*

Centre: Men of the US 82nd Airborne Division at Cottesmore, England, about to board their gliders on 17 September. The soldier with the map is armed with an M1 Garand rifle and on the ground to the right is an M1 Carbine. *(IWM EA.37782)*

Below: A CG-4A glider of the US 101st Airborne Division has the finishing touches applied to its nose decoration by its pilot before the launch of Operation Market Garden. *(ASOMF)*

A C-47 Dakota tugs a US 101st Airborne Division CG-4A glider into the air on 17 September. These men were flown into Holland on the southern route and were watched by the men of the Guards Armoured Division as their aircraft flew over the Meuse-Escaut canal. *(IWM EA.37974)*

A view from Belgium in the early afternoon of 17 September showing C-47 transport aircraft carrying the US 101st Airborne Division into Holland. *(IWM B.10111)*

road towards Arnhem, making it clear to all concerned that the airborne troops would remain highly vulnerable until union had been established with them. His audience understood that the success of the operation was as much in their hands as it was in those of the airborne forces, but also knew that, based on their recent experiences, it was extremely likely the enemy would fight hard and do all that they could to stop them from attaining the momentum that they required to keep to their tight schedule. Nevertheless, Horrocks's confidence was infectious and few doubted that they would not make their rendezvous with the three airborne divisions in good time. The XXX Corps commander was experienced, modest and showed a remarkable degree of humility for a soldier that had achieved such a high rank. Well known and liked by Montgomery, as they had fought together in the Western Desert, Horrocks was an extremely capable commander, but he had been badly wounded in Italy and in September 1944 was still weak and sometimes relapsed into illness. This physical difficulty may or may not have had a bearing upon Horrocks's style of command during the North West Europe Campaign in September 1944, but it was symptomatic of a growing problem within XXX Corps, that his troops – consisting of the Guards Armoured, 43rd and 50th Divisions, together with the 4th Armoured Brigade and the Princess Irene Brigade of Free Dutch – were tired, short of manpower and, with the war coming to its conclusion, lacking the 'bite' they had displayed while trying to establish themselves in France a few months earlier. In such circumstances it was at least true that XXX Corps were in a position to put their hard-won and valuable experience to use in the planning and execution of Operation Garden. However, fighting 20,000 vehicles down one single road was a major concern for its commanders, for while there was an understandable emphasis on the need for speed, Holland, with its water-logged landscape, numerous bridges and waterways, seemed to provide the Germans with great defensive advantages. In such circumstances it was therefore crucial that the ground forces had the resources with which to combat the likelihood of the enemy destroying vital bridges that were required if they were to make any

Above: The air armada for the first lift of US 82nd Airborne Division troops. These C-47s had a maximum speed of 230 mph at 8,500 feet and a cruising speed of 185 mph. These aircraft were so reliable and versatile that the last was not withdrawn from service with the RAF until 1970. *(IWM EA.74538)*

Left: The air armada en route for Holland on 17 September. A total of 143 C-47s of the American 61st and 314th Troop Carrier Groups transported the first lift troops of the British 1st Airborne Division with the first take off at 0945 hr. *(IWM NYF.60657)*

A Horsa glider being towed behind a Stirling on its way to LZ 'Z' on 17 September. The Horsa was operated by two pilots sitting next to each other and had a towing speed of 130–140 knots, a gliding speed of 100 knots and a landing speed of 70–80 knots. (J. Falconer)

A 295 Squadron Short Stirling returning to RAF Harwell from Arnhem during the afternoon of 17 September. No Stirlings were lost on this day, but forty-eight were lost in the course of the battle during low altitude resupply missions. (J. Falconer)

further progress towards Arnhem. To this end bridging materials were made readily available to the attacking corps and were sensibly situated near the front of the column together with 2,300 specialist vehicles and 9,000 sappers and pioneers. Whether such precautions were sufficient for the task very much depended on how quickly the Germans reacted to Operation Market and the time that it took for the ground forces to link up with their airborne colleagues.

Leading the charge for XXX Corps at the head of the Guards Armoured Division were the Irish Guards Group. These tough and experienced troops prepared to advance while, at 1245 hr, Allied fighters prepared the battlefield for them with accurate low-level attacks onto German positions. At 1400 hr the devastation wrought by the aircraft was followed with a bombardment by 350 British

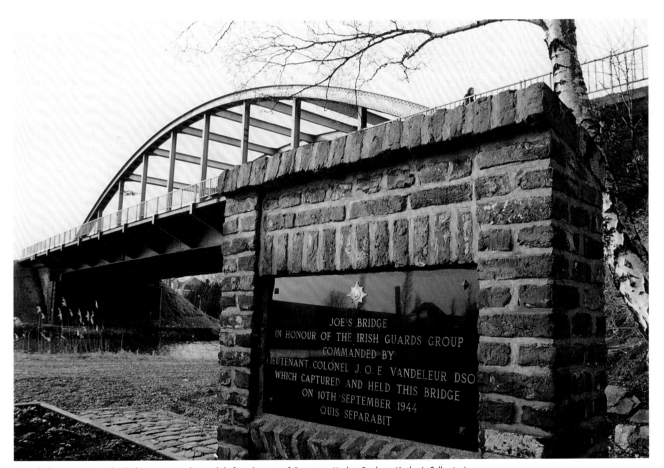

'Joe's bridge' near Neerpelt which was captured a week before the start of Operation Market Garden. *(Author's Collection)*

The 25-pounders of 430 Battery, 55th RA Field Regiment, firing in support of the breakout from the bridgehead over the Meuse-Escaut canal by the Guards Armoured Division on 17 September. *(IWM B.9986)*

guns aimed primarily at the enemy's gun and troops concentrations. When this was finished, the guns then laid down a barrage 400 yards ahead of the British front line and 1000 yards on either side of the road. At 1435 hr, this barrage crept forward and behind it the Irish Guards advanced supported by a battalion of the 50th Division and some rocket-firing Typhoons providing close air support. However, although this firepower did weaken the German defences, large numbers of the enemy and their weapons survived. These troops, men of Kampfgruppe Walther's crack 6th Parachute Regiment, waited anxiously in whatever cover could be found nearby as the artillery barrage swept over, then resumed their positions and waited for the enemy to move into range. The slow moving British convoy advanced towards them, the infantry mounted on the armour behind the lead elements, and then when they were in killing range, the Germans opened fire with their anti-tank guns and *panzerfausts* and knocked out nine of the lead tanks. With the Shermans on fire and the rattle of German machine guns in their ears, the British infantry immediately dismounted and scattered into the fields on either side of the road. Aided by Typhoons, these troops then moved deftly towards the German positions, overran them and cleared the area. The fighting caused a delay in the advance, but such hiatuses were expected when penetrating what was a tough German defensive 'crust'. But it was also expected that the initial resistance had been overcome, so that the going would be more conducive to the speedy relief of the airborne forces. Nevertheless, this initial engagement revealed to the commanders of both sides that it would not be particularly difficult for XXX Corps to be delayed at any point along the long road to Arnhem as long as sufficient force was brought to bear on them. The force just beyond the Meuse-Escaut canal was sufficient enough to delay the arrival of the vanguard of XXX Corps in the town of Valkenswaard until 1930 hr. Although they were only some 6 miles south of their scheduled stop in Eindhoven, here the Guards Armoured Division halted for the night. The decision not to push on was not well received by the division, despite their exertions of the day, but it was believed that the risk of advancing into an enemy-held city at night out-weighed its potential

A British military cemetery close to the start line for Operation Market Garden containing the graves of many officers and men of the Irish Guards. *(Author's Collection)*

benefits, and so stop they did. It seems that even at this early stage in the operation, an extremely cautious hand held the reigns of XXX Corps, and this hand set a pace which did not over exert its weary units. The advance had begun, but Horrocks's men were already behind schedule and few believed that this was an operation in which lost time could be made up later on.

As the Irish Guards made their preparations for a night in Valkenswaard, the British and American airborne forces that had landed extremely successfully in Holland that afternoon, had also engaged with the enemy as they endeavoured to secure their objectives. In the Arnhem sector there were six areas designated as DZs and LZs for Urquhart's 1st Airborne Division which, in common with its American counterparts, was scheduled to be lifted into Holland over three days. In the first lift, a total of 5,700 men, were the 1st Parachute Brigade, commanded by Brig Gerald Lathbury, which was to move into Arnhem immediately after landing and seize three crossing points over the Lower Rhine – a railway bridge, a pontoon bridge and, the main objective, the main road

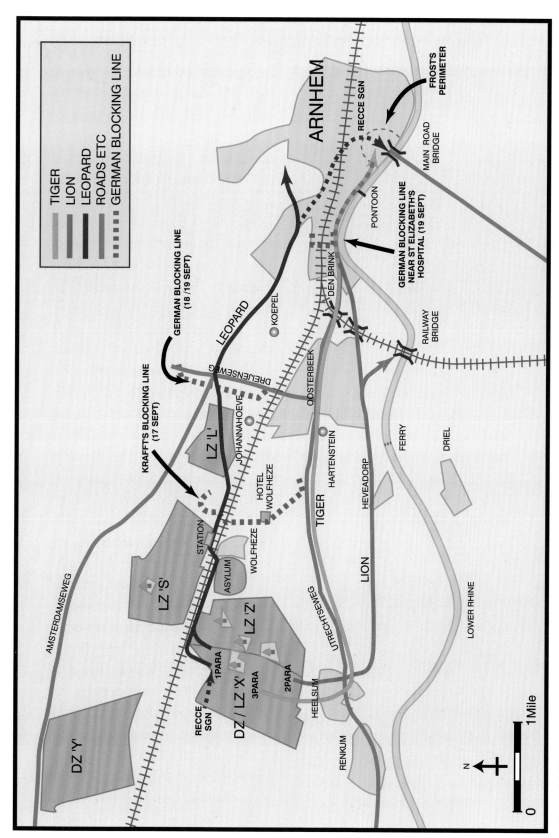

Arnhem Battlefield, 17–19 September 1944.

Brig Gerald Lathbury, commander of the 1st Parachute Brigade, which contained many experienced airborne soldiers and arrived in Holland with the first lift on 17 September. *(IWM H.40924)*

bridge – together with an area of high ground around the north of Arnhem that was to be used to defend against German counter-attacks. The brigade consisted of 1st Parachute Battalion (1Para), commanded by Lt Col David Dobie; 2nd Parachute Battalion (2Para) commanded by Lt Col John Frost and 3rd Parachute Battalion (3Para), commanded by Lt Col John Fitch. Also arriving on 17 September, along with Urquhart's divisional head-quarters and two-thirds of his 75-mm field artillery, was the bulk of the 1st Airlanding Brigade, commanded by Brig Philip Hicks. This brigade, consisting of 1st Battalion the Border Regiment; 7th Battalion the King's Own Scottish Borderers and the 2nd Battalion South Staffordshires, had been tasked with holding the DZs and LZs for the subsequent lifts before moving into Arnhem itself. In the second lift Brigadier John 'Shan' Hackett's 4th Parachute Brigade would arrive and these three parachute regiment battalions were to link up with Lathbury's men and defend a 12-mile long perimeter around Arnhem against German counter-attacks. The third lift, consisting of Sosabowski's 1st Polish Independent Parachute Brigade, was to provide reinforcements.

The first men of the division to touch down outside Arnhem were from the 21st Independent Parachute Company who parachuted into the DZs and LZs 20 minutes before the main

Montgomery at Oakham in March 1944 with the commander of the 4th Parachute Brigade, Brig J.W. Hackett (in the middle of the group), and Maj Gen R.E. Urquhart. *(IWM H36611)*

force. This unit worked quickly without interference from the enemy and laid out indicator panels, set off smoke signals and switched on Eureka homing beacons in order to guide aircraft accurately to their destinations. At 1300 hr 134 gliders of the infantry of the airlanding brigade began to land on LZ 'S' and shortly after, 150 gliders containing the divisional headquarters, the jeeps of the Reconnaissance Squadron, some of the light guns and supporting troops, landed on LZ 'Z'. In the minutes immediately after 1350 hr, 2,278 canopies opened over DZ 'X' announcing the arrival of the 1st Parachute Brigade. Jumping from 500 ft and in the air for just a few seconds, these parachutists, in common with the glider-borne troops, encountered only very limited enemy opposition as they landed with the few Germans who did not run away at the first sight of the airborne troops, being overrun or surrendering before they could do much damage. On landing, these airborne troops immediately made for their rendezvous points and then, after a delay of approximately 90 minutes in which they organised themselves, the parachute battalions moved off eastwards towards Arnhem and the airlanding infantry dispersed to prepare their defences in anticipation of the second lift.

Lt Col John Frost, Commanding Officer of 2Para during Operation Market Garden. The battalion was formed on 1 October 1941 and Frost commanded one of its companies in the successful Bruneval Raid. Later he led 2Para in North Africa, and by September 1944 was the most experienced battalion commander in the British 1st Airborne Division. *(IWM BU.10524)*

The attack in this part of Holland came as a complete surprise to the German commanders in the area, including Model whose headquarters was at the Hotel Tafelberg in Oosterbeek just a couple of miles from the British landings on the road to Arnhem. This was extraordinarily bad luck for Urquhart, for as Model fled, initially believing in the confusion that he was the objective of the attack, he

Above: The parachutes of the US 82nd Airborne Division opening over the Groesbeek Heights on the afternoon of 17 September. This ground was deemed vital by Browning, and his controversial decision to declare it the division's priority severely hampered Gavin's ability to provide enough men for an early attack on the Nijmegen bridges. *(IWM EA.38796)*

Opposite, top: US 82nd Airborne Division parachutists fill the sky after jumping from their Douglas C-47 Dakotas. Their commander, Brig Gen James Gavin, said that the drop in Holland on 17 September 'was better than had ever been experienced'. *(IWM EA.39925)*

Opposite, bottom left: DZ 'X' looking south-east as 1st Parachute Brigade began to jump from their C-47s. Each of the three parachute battalions arrived in 34 C-47s; divisional HQ in 7; brigade HQ in 9; 1 Parachute Squadron Royal Engineers in 9 and 16 Parachute Field Ambulances in 6 each. A total of 2,278 men were dropped here on 17 September. *(IWM CL.1168)*

Centre: LZ 'Z' looking north on the afternoon of 17 September with the railway line — bordered by trees — emerging from the top left of the picture and stretching across to the right with LZ 'S' beyond it. A total of 284 gliders landed on these two LZs on the first day. The Germans destroyed all the gliders after the battle. *(IWM CL.1172)*

Below: The RV point of 1Para on DZ 'X' on 17 September looking north. At the end of the road on the right is the railway line. *(Author's Collection)*

The Horsa gliders containing the headquarters of the 1st Airlanding Light Regiment, RA. The CO, Lt Col 'Sheriff' Thompson, can be seen carrying haversacks as a signalman endeavours to make contact with other units in the vehicle behind him. (IWM BU.1164)

Looking north-west across LZ 'Z' and DZ 'X' near Wolfheze at around 1300 hr on 17 September as paratroopers began to drop. The gliders that can be seen are Horsas which were the army's first troop-carrying gliders with a length of 67 feet and a span of 88 feet. The Horsa could carry between twenty-six and twenty-nine troops or light guns, jeeps or trailers and could have, as can be seen, a quick release tail unit for ease of unloading. (IWM

Men of 1st Airlanding Brigade preparing for the defence of DZ 'X', which was to become LZ 'X' for the second lift. These soldiers are armed with .303 Lee Enfield rifles and 9mm Stens. The later were unreliable, but could be excellent for house clearance and close quarters fighting. *(IWM BU.1124)*

left orders with the commandant of Arnhem, Gen Kussin, and then headed for the headquarters of II SS Panzer Corps at Doetinchem, 25 miles to the east. Model's actions, together with those of his subordinate commanders, show that the Germans recovered quickly from the surprise of the assault and reacted immediately to the perceived threats. This situation was, ironically, compounded by the success of the compact and accurate daylight landings, which, although allowing the airborne forces to concentrate immediately for an attack towards their objectives, also allowed the German defenders to deploy their forces between the British and their most likely objectives in Arnhem.

The distances from DZs and LZs to the bridges were one important part of the plan that gave Urquhart and his commanders great cause for concern. They compounded British problems as the distances gave the Germans the time that they needed to assess the situation and set up crucial blocking positions. German reaction to the British at the northern end of the Market Garden corridor was admirably swift, but Model's colleagues further to the south were also impressively responsive and were rapidly incorporated into a defensive plan. Aided by the acquisition of a copy of the Allied operational order that had been found on the body of a dead

The Tafelberg Hotel – Model's headquarters as the 1st British Airborne Division began to drop on 17 September, and later used by the British as a main dressing station. (Author's Collection)

American airborne officer close to Student's headquarters that afternoon, Model divided the area under attack into three zones. The defensive plan required Student to deal with the advancing XXX Corps and the 101st Airborne Division around Eindhoven; Wehrkreis VI, containing Corps Feldt and 40th Division, to tackle the 82nd Airborne Division, and Christiansen to counter-attack the British around Arnhem using II SS Panzer Corps and Kampfgruppe von Tettau, which included SS-Captain Sepp Krafft's SS Training and Depot Battalion. It was Krafft's 36 officers and NCOs and their 349 half-trained young soldiers with their 88-mm guns, mortars, machine guns and flamethrowers, that elements of the 1st Parachute Brigade were to immediately run into as they pushed into Arnhem. Bittrich also moved quickly to stave off a crisis and ordered the 9th SS Panzer Division to deal with the British in and around Arnhem, and the 10th SS Panzer Division to cross the Arnhem bridge, sweep south and defend the crossings over the Waal at Nijmegen. It took some time for these two dispersed divisions to assemble before moving off towards their objectives, but as they organised themselves Harzer's reconnaissance battalion was ordered to reconnoitre into Nijmegen in an attempt to forestall any initial American attempt to seize the bridges there.

As Bittrich's forces raced to intercept both the British and American attacks on the crucial river crossings, the 1st Parachute Brigade began its advance. The three battalions of the brigade took separate routes into Arnhem: the northern route, codenamed 'Leopard', ran along the Amsterdamseweg and was to take 1Para to the high ground; 'Tiger' route, to its south, was to take 3Para into Arnhem along the Utrechtseweg, and 2Para's 'Lion' route ran alongside the Lower Rhine past the railway bridge, the pontoon bridge and directly to the main road bridge. Urquhart was well aware of the dangers in diluting the brigade in such close terrain, but he thought that the potential problems

The Reconnaissance Squadron's route from their LZ on the first day to Wolfheze, taken from the just by the Wolfheze level crossing. *(Author's Collection)*

The Wolfheze level crossing looking north-east. It was across this railway line that the Reconnaissance Squadron drove on the afternoon of 17 September before turning right just beyond it and running into a German ambush. *(Author's Collection)*

Men of 1Para take cover in a shell hole near Wolfheze during the afternoon of the 17th. It is likely that this damage had been caused by Allied bombing the previous evening. The man on the extreme left is armed with a .303 Bren gun. These were excellent light support weapons and each section was issued with at least one. *(IWM BU.1167)*

German prisoners being taken to a holding point near Wolfheze. Unfortunately for the airborne troops they had few resources with which to administer these prisoners, as they could not pass them out of the 1st Airborne Division's area of operations until XXX Corps had linked up with them. *(IWM BU.1166)*

The dead driver of Gen Kussin's staff car which was ambushed by the lead platoon of 3Para as it sped on to the Utrechtseweg, having just left SS Capt Sepp Krafft's headquarters at Hotel Wolfheze. *(IWM BU.1156)*

in doing so were outweighed by the likelihood that at least one of the routes would provide ready access into Arnhem, and that the brigade would not be stretched out along just one road. Moreover, he believed that the converging forces of two battalions could more rapidly reinforce Gough's Reconnaissance Squadron *coup de main* force at the main Arnhem bridge, and that 1Para would inevitably benefit from taking the shortest route to the high ground.

Urquhart's planning was clear and based on sound reasoning, but from the outset things started to go wrong, proving that plans rarely survive first contact with the enemy. The Reconnaissance Squadron was late setting off towards Arnhem from its rendezvous point and by the time that it was eventually speeding towards the bridge, it slammed into the waiting German defenders just east of the Wolfheze crossroads and was immediately halted. Gough's men had been ambushed from positions at the northern end of Krafft's blocking position, which extended along the line of the Oosterbeek–Wolfheze road, completely cutting Leopard route and touching Tiger route at its southern extremity. The result was that there was no speedy seizure of the Arnhem road bridge and 1 and 3Para could make only limited progress towards their objectives on the first day. Dobie's men ran into some German armour and infantry on Leopard route and were forced into trying to find a way to outflank it. Heading into the woods to the south that evening the battalion ran into more Germans and took some heavy casualties without finding any way through. Fitch's men on the Utrechtseweg, meanwhile, managed to skirt underneath Krafft's blocking position, but were then delayed twice and suffered some casualties when they contacted some Germans making good use of the cover provided by the numerous buildings in the vicinity. 3Para's lead platoon had, however, killed Gen Kussin, whose staff car was riddled with bullets as it tried to turn onto the Utrechtseweg, having just left Krafft's headquarters at the Hotel Wolfheze on the Oosterbeek-Wolfheze road. This was undoubtedly a blow for the Germans, but by nightfall 3Para were still some 800 yards short of the Hartenstein Hotel in Oosterbeek and unsure what lay ahead of them. Krafft had done an exceptionally good job slowing the advance of 1st Parachute Brigade thus gaining important time for other units, including 9th SS Panzer Division, to deploy. His blocking position had turned the tables on the 1st Airborne Division and caused confusion and consternation while exposing the flaws in their plan.

Unfortunately for the British, Urquhart, despite the proximity of his headquarters near Wolfheze to the fighting, was unable to influence the rapidly developing situation as his communications had failed. After a protracted and frustrating period, during which

The Lower Rhine near the Driel ferry.
(Author's Collection)

The view eastwards from the Westerbouwing Heights. In the extreme distance on the left, the arch of Arnhem bridge can be seen. In the near distance is the Arnhem railway bridge. (Author's Collection)

he could hear fighting, but could not contact Lathbury's brigade or the headquarters of the Airborne Corps near Nijmegen, Urquhart took a bold decision and sped off in a jeep in the direction of Arnhem. The divisional commander's decision to personally find out what was happening to 1st Parachute Brigade was a calculated risk but, quite obviously, should not have been necessary. Adequate communications are essential on any battlefield, but they are of even greater importance when isolated, vulnerable and fragmented airborne forces meet unexpected enemy opposition. The communication difficulties that blighted the British airborne division came about as the result of several factors, not least the inadequate ranges of the sets in the wooded and built up terrain, a situation that could have been avoided had more powerful sets been made more widely available to them. Urquhart's troops were not helped by a plan that had many obvious frailties, inevitable perhaps in the circumstances, but there was no excuse for them having to deploy with inadequate equipment.

By the time that Urquhart had begun to fret about the progress being made towards Arnhem and 1 and 3Para had run into some stubborn enemy resistance, 2Para, followed by brigade headquarters, had already made their way through the outskirts of Heelsum and on to Lion route. Frost's men had been delayed by a throng of Dutch locals who clogged the road in their joy to welcome their liberators, but when officers and NCOs heard the unmistakable sound of battle to their north, they encouraged their men to make haste and to be

German defensive preparations to the west of Arnhem. Although it is known that this picture dates from the battle, it is impossible to determine exactly where and when it was taken (although from the leisurely attitude of troops it would seem unlikely that British troops were in the immediate vicinity of these trenches). *(IWM MH.3956)*

aware of the dangers that could lurk in the houses and woods before them. 2Para pressed on towards Arnhem relatively unhindered by the enemy, except for a few snipers, and one company slipped off the road to seize the railway bridge across the Lower Rhine just to the south of Oosterbeek. However, as the first men stepped on to the bridge, the Germans destroyed it. The demolition of the bridge might not have had such important repercussions had the pontoon bridge been found in one piece, but the Germans had already dismantled it and with it British desires to take the Arnhem bridge from both ends simultaneously. In such circumstances the Heveadorp ferry across the Lower Rhine, linking Westerbouwing, their the south bank, to the east of Driel, would have been a potential solution to the river crossing problem, but its importance had been overlooked during the planning stages of the operation and so, despite the fact that it was adjacent to the river road, it did not become a designated 2Para objective. In fact the ferry does not seem to have warranted the attention that it deserved, even after an officer during the evening of the 17th brought its existence to the attention of divisional headquarters. As nothing was done to utilise the ferry, it was eventually made unusable by a well meaning local who, surprised by the apparent lack of British interest in it, cut is moorings so as to deny the Germans use of it.

Urquhart's jeep followed the 2Para route as the general probed forward on his fact-finding mission, and he soon came across the battalion's tail. Demanding greater urgency of the officers that he found there, but confident that the battalion was at least moving forward, Urquhart wasted no time and headed off to the north to see what the situation was on 3Para's Tiger route. On reaching the cobbled Utrechtseweg, Urquhart came across Lathbury who had also left his headquarters in an attempt to find out what was happening to his brigade after his own communications failure. What was immediately apparent to the two men was that 3Para had encountered the enemy up ahead but it was decided, was being far too cautious and needed to make some sacrifices for the sake of greater speed. However, with darkness falling and communication impossible, the chances of accelerating the battalion at that time were not good. Urquhart's mood was grim, for the battle was not going to plan and both he and Lathbury had become separated from their headquarters and were unable to influence the battle. However, with the enemy closing in and the situation confused, they had little option but remain with 3Para until daylight and brood on their problems.

In their peculiar circumstances and with no radio communication available to them, neither Urquhart nor Lathbury had any idea that

An 82nd Airborne Division memorial near Overasselt on DZ 'O' (504th PIR). *(Author's Collection)*

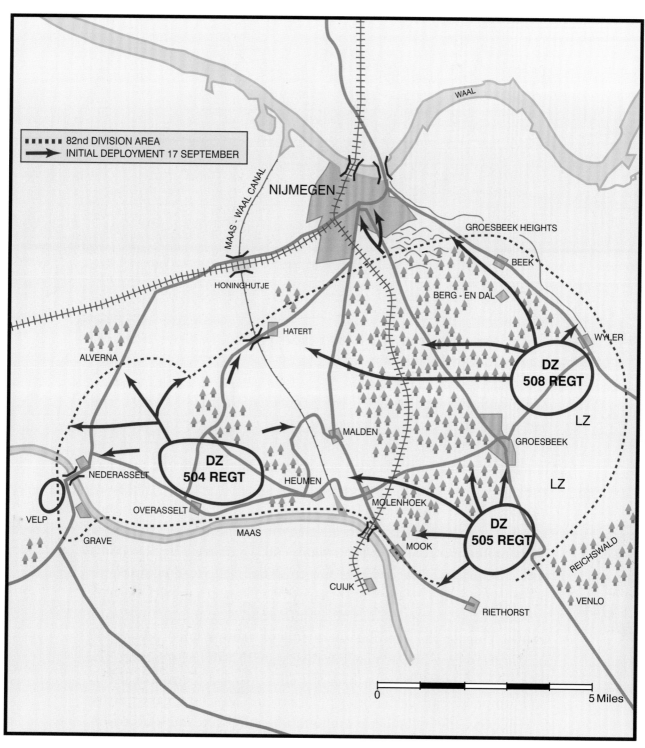

82nd Airborne Division Plan.

The southern end of the bridge at Grave being crossed by a T-16 carrier and some XXX Corps trucks as locals look on. The flood plain of the Maas can be clearly seen to the right of the picture. *(IWM B.10344)*

2Para had managed to reach the Arnhem road bridge at dusk and had found it deserted. Although Frost's leading company had been held up by German small arms fire as they moved through the immediate outskirts of Arnhem at a place called Den Brink, they had managed to outflank the position and pushed on. At the bridge buildings were immediately taken over by 1st Parachute Brigade Headquarters and 2Para, and a defensive position was established enabling the protection of its northern end. Units were deployed in a way that allowed clear fields of fire on to the ramp leading up to the main span of the bridge in anticipation of an attempted German crossing at some time – but the southern end remained in enemy hands. During the evening the airborne troops tried on several occasions to cross the bridge, but they were thwarted each time. The first attempt failed when a hail of bullets from a German pill box and armoured car on the bridge cut into the attacking parachutists. The pill box and an adjacent ammunition store were later destroyed, but the fire from them ignited the paint on the girders and the subsequent illumination of the bridge undermined later assaults. The

Germans then counter-attacked, but a probe from the eastern side of Frost's perimeter was contained and four lorries that tried to cross into Arnhem from the southern end of the bridge were quickly despatched. Throughout this period of intermittent action, increasing numbers of British airborne troops managed to get through to join Frost's perimeter, including a number of Royal Engineers, a platoon of the Royal Army Service Corps, Gough with a small part of his force and part of 3Para's 'C' Company, which had managed to seep through the German blocking positions in Oosterbeek. By the early hours of Monday 18 September some 750 men out of the anticipated 2,000 had managed to get through to the Arnhem bridge.

Operation Market Garden was not just about Arnhem, however, for while the British landed north of the Lower Rhine in the early afternoon of 17 September, the 82nd Airborne Division were doing the same some 15 miles to the south. Gavin's division had the onerous task of capturing the road and rail bridges over the Waal in Nijmegen, the bridge over the Maas at Grave, the bridges over the Maas-Waal canal and securing the Groesbeek Heights, which bordered the Reichswald. Three parachute infantry regiments and a little artillery were to drop in the first lift, the balance of the division's artillery was to land in the second lift, and the glider infantry with the third lift. One of the division's designated DZs was to the south-west of Nijmegen and here Col Reuben H. Tucker's 504th Parachute Infantry was to land. Their wide-ranging tasks included the seizing of the northern end of the Grave bridge over the Maas, the capture of the Honinghutje, Malden and Heumen bridges over the Maas-Waal canal, and prevention of any ground being lost to German counter-attacks from the west. Another company of the 504th was to be dropped at the southern end of the Grave bridge in order to facilitate the seizing of both ends of this crucial crossing simultaneously. The final 82nd Airborne Division DZ was to the south-east of Nijmegen not far from the Reichswald. It was here that Col Roy E. Lindquist's 508th Parachute Infantry, Col William E. Ekman's 505th Parachute Infantry, the divisional headquarters and eight 75-mm guns were to be inserted. The 505th were to drop

A memorial to the men of the 101st Airborne Division who successfully captured the Grave bridge. *(Author's Collection)*

south of Groesbeek, take the village and the ridge down to Kiekberg, while patrols helped in the attempts to take the bridges over the Maas-Waal canal at Heuman and Malden. The 508th were to drop to the north of Groesbeek and were to defend a 6-mile sector from Berg en Dal south to Groesbeek. The 508th, it was decided just before take off, would also provide a battalion to strike out for the Nijmegen bridges if, and it was a very important if, they were not required elsewhere that afternoon.

These men were the only troops provided for by the plan to try and seize the Waal crossings that day. Quite clearly the decision not to send other units to help in the capture of the bridges reflected the prioritisation of divisional objectives. As resources were so scant and being entirely realistic, Gavin thought it was likely that the bridges would not be taken without the help of the Guards Armoured Division. This potential time delay between the arrival of the airborne troops and the arrival of XXX Corps, however, led to the distinct possibility that the Germans would have time to either destroy the bridges, leaving a 1,960-foot gap to span, or establish strong defensive positions to protect their southern approaches. Nevertheless, Browning believed that it was crucial to capture and secure the Groesbeek Heights before a push on the bridges could be made. The plan reflected this, because he felt that the high ground was potentially vulnerable to an armoured counter-attack out of the Reichswald which, if successful, would allow the Germans to see into the heart of Nijmegen and, crucially, observe the bridges. The Corps commander wrote to this end in an operational order: 'The capture and retention of the high ground between Nijmegen and

Groesbeek is imperative in order to accomplish the Division's task.' In reality, however, Gavin need not have been ordered to secure such a large proportion of the high ground, as the crucial Nijmegen road bridge could not, in fact, be seen from the high ground 2 miles to its east, and so the valuable troops that had been tasked with the securing of this area could have been released to tackle one or both of the Waal crossings. Even so, Browning remained confident that the bridges would be taken intact and on time, indeed he even demanded valuable glider assets to deliver his own headquarters to Groesbeek on the first day of operations.

On the 17th Gavin's first lift of around 7,500 men successfully landed south of the Waal. The drops were accurate with only 2 per cent jump casualties and the few Germans that were encountered near the DZs were quickly overcome. The 504th began to land on Dutch soil around both ends of the Grave bridge at around 1315 hr. At the southern end most of the company landed approximately 1 mile away, but 1 stick of 16 men touched down just 800 yards from the bridge and immediately rushed their objective. The crossing was also attacked from the north end with the result that the bridge was secured before its startled German defenders had a chance to detonate their charges. The rest of the day was spent by this part of the 504th in consolidating the area around the bridge and taking the

The bridge at Grave looking north. Units from the 101st Airborne Division landed on ground behind where this picture was taken and stormed the southern end. (Author's Collection)

An American glider loading jeeps through its open nose in preparation for the US 82nd Airborne Division's first lift to Holland on 17 September. These vehicles gave the airborne troops much needed mobility on the battlefield and could be used to transport heavy equipment quickly and efficiently. *(ASOMF)*

village of Grave, which was vacated by its 400 German occupants later that afternoon. Of the other two battalions of the regiment, one cleared the enemy from the area between the Maas and the Maas-Waal canal while the other endeavoured to take the bridges at Heumen and Malden. An intact crossing over the canal was crucial, not just so that XXX Corps had a route into Nijmegen, but also so that the 504th were not cut off from the rest of the division further to the east. One company was sent to seize each of the two bridges, but although the Malden bridge was destroyed as the paratroopers approached it, the Heumen bridge was taken after an exchange of small arms fire and a charge by the Americans. Three of these men made it across the bridge to the eastern side, where they were quickly reinforced by seven others who crossed the canal in a small rowing boat, and the area was speedily consolidated. It was this bridge that was to become the main crossing point for XXX Corps after the other bridges over the waterway had all been destroyed by the Germans. The Mook crossing was blown up before the 505th could take it on the 17th, the same happened to the Hatert bridge that day as it was attacked by a combined force of the 504th and 508th, and the Honinghutje bridge was rendered impassable to heavy traffic on the morning of the 18th when men of the 508th tried to storm it. The Heumen bridge was, therefore, the vital link.

The 508th Parachute Infantry Regiment spread themselves over a wide area once they had landed. One battalion moved to Hatert to take up positions astride the Nijmegen-Mook road to block any German counter-attacks pushing south out of Nijmegen and threatening any of the crossings captured over the Maas-Waal canal. It was this battalion which sent a platoon to unsuccessfully capture the Hatert bridge on the 17th and on the following day sent another two platoons on an equally abortive attack on the Honinghutje bridge. The second battalion moved into defensive positions along a 3½-mile stretch of the ridge line which stretched from the south east of Nijmegen to Berg-en-Dal. These troops were deployed to block any enemy movement from the east which threatened the southern and eastern approaches to Nijmegen and to deny the Germans the high ground which, apart from being required by the division for their subsequent lifts, also supposedly offered the Germans excellent observation into Nijmegen. This battalion managed to capture Berg-en-Dal by nightfall, but they failed in their attempts to cut the road from Nijmegen to Kleve and consequently prepared themselves for another attempt on the following day. The third battalion of the 508th, commanded by Lt Col Shields Warren Jnr, was the unit tasked with tackling the Nijmegen road bridge if and when circumstances were conducive for them to do so. After landing, Warren's battalion moved quickly to its first objective near De Ploeg, just over 1 mile to the south-east of the city, and here they waited until it was certain that they were not required elsewhere. Eventually, in the early evening, a reconnaissance patrol was sent forward to scout ahead and obtain information about the situation in Nijmegen. Just like the British in Arnhem, however, communication problems meant that this small force lost contact with its parent body until the next morning, and so the battalion had to enter the city without crucial intelligence. A local man was found to guide one company through the maze of streets to the main road bridge at around 2000 hr, but another company got lost en route to their objective. The fog of war had fallen suddenly on the 508th, fragmenting it and masking what lay ahead. What this company did know as they approached the bridge, however, was that whatever Germans had been in and around the city that afternoon had probably been organised into some strong defensive positions by that stage, and that the delay in sending them into the city could have unfortunate repercussions for XXX Corp's attempt to get to Arnhem quickly.

As the American parachutists reached the Keizer Karel Plein, a roundabout approximately 1 mile south-west of the southern end of the road bridge, at about 2200 hr, their fears were realised when they ran into strong enemy positions which were being busily reinforced. Had an attack on the bridge been made earlier, the parachutists would have encountered some disorganised second rate troops, instead they waited, and the small force ran into the newly arrived men of the 9th SS Reconnaissance Battalion, sent to Nijmegen that afternoon by Bittrich. As the Americans began to probe forward at the Keizer Karel Plein, the quality of the defending German troops became immediately apparent to them. Professional, tenacious and well led, the defenders of Nijmegen bridge would be extremely difficult to crack and even at this early stage in the battle it looked as if Gavin's prediction that the bridge would remain in enemy hands until XXX Corps arrived would be correct. Still without the support of the other company, the parachutists struggled to find any way round or through these strong German positions and were eventually forced to withdraw and seek reinforcement.

The difficulty was, however, that even though the bridges would be destroyed by the Germans at any moment, reinforcements were not readily available. There was little that the local commanders could do about augmenting their numbers, but they did try to thwart German attempts to disable the bridge after they received information from the locals, erroneous information it later turned

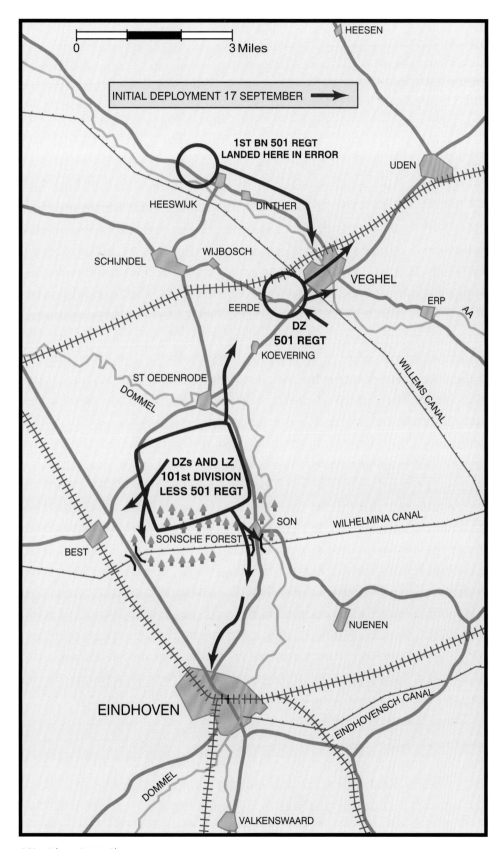

101st Airborne Division Plan.

out, that the control mechanism for detonating the charges on the road bridge was to be found in the main post office just 400 yd to the east of the roundabout. A platoon was despatched to check whether the information was correct and if it was to destroy the mechanism with all possible haste. The small force fought their way to the Post Office and put the machinery that they found there out of action and then tried to return to the main group, but found that they had been surrounded. These men, together with some locals who were helping them, held out for three days before being relieved. Warren, meanwhile, tried to do what he could with his limited resources to put pressure on the enemy at the roundabout by using fire and manoeuvre, but the Germans skilfully counter-attacked before dawn, and by daylight it was not the men of the 9th SS Division who were in an invidious situation, but the Americans.

One of the reasons why the attack into Nijmegen by the 508th was eventually approved during the early evening of 17 September was because the 505th Parachute Infantry, dropping on the most southerly DZ on the high ground, had not encountered the much-feared German armoured opposition that had been predicted by some. Having landed in good order and sent patrols to establish what, if any, the enemy threat was from the Reichswald, the regiment soon came to the conclusion that any German opposition from the east would not be strong in the short term. Nevertheless, defensive positions were established as a precaution and one battalion dug in just to the north of Groesbeek, another took the village and then occupied the ridge to its west (and linked up with the 504th around Heumen), and the third battalion deployed on the ridge further to the south and successfully captured Kiekberg and Riethorst. However, attempts by a party from this battalion to capture the bridge at Mook failed when its defenders destroyed it.

The 82nd Airborne Division achieved a great deal on the first afternoon that was of value for a successful conclusion to Operation Market Garden, not least the taking of bridges over the Maas and Maas-Waal canal. But there was still the vital crossing over the Waal to capture, and unless this was done in time to effect a link with the British at Arnhem, the efforts of the 101st Airborne Division further

These men were among the first US airborne troops to land in Holland on 17 September and are greeted by Dutch locals. This soldier is armed with an M1 .30-calibre rifle commonly called the Garand. The rifle had a robust design, was accurate at long range and had a semi-automatic action. *(IWM EA.38132)*

to the south would be in vain. In common with the other two divisional airborne commanders on 17 September, Maxwell Taylor knew as he flew to Holland that his resources would be spread extremely thinly if he was to be successful in all that he had been asked to achieve. The task allotted to the division was to secure the main road for the advance of XXX Corps between Eindhoven and Veghel and with it, the bridges over the Wilhelmina canal at Son, the Dommel at St Oedenrode and the Zuid Willems canal and Aa at Veghel. Despite the fact that the 101st were to receive the largest share of the first lift, Taylor was concerned that his division would face the stiffest German opposition on landing, for they would be relatively close to the front line. Moreover, he also did not relish the prospect of having to defend so many bridges and 15 miles of exposed road between Eindhoven and Nijmegen even after union had been made with XXX Corps. 101st Airborne Division commanders were particularly worried about early German armoured attacks, as their artillery was not due to arrive until the second lift and their glider infantry with the third. The wait, many believed, would be an anxious one, especially if XXX Corps were slow in arriving.

Paratroopers of the US 101st Airborne
Division jump from their C-47s on
17 September 1944. *(ASOMF)*

The main DZ for the division was approximately 1 mile north-
west of the Son bridge, and here both the 502nd and 506th
Parachute Infantry Regiments were to be dropped. Further to the
north were two smaller designated DZs, one either side of the Zuid
Willems canal and Aa river so that their bridges could be taken from
both ends simultaneously. Here two battalions of the 501st
Parachute Infantry Regiment were to be dropped, one just to the
south-west of Veghel, and the battalion just to the north-west of the
town. In the thirty minutes after 1300 hr on 17 September a total of
6,769 parachutists of the 101st, together with attached supporting
units arriving in gliders, landed in Holland. Col Robert Sink's 506th
Parachute Infantry landed safely and promptly moved south to
secure the Son bridge and establish union with the Guards
Armoured Division in the city of Eindhoven. Sink would have
preferred to have dropped his men on either side of the Wilhelmina
canal so that the crossing could have been attacked from the south
side as well as from the north, but the strength of the anticipated
flak emanating from Eindhoven precluded this and so the speed of
the battalion to the bridge was all the more essential. The village of

Son, just north of the crossing, was entered by the 506th quickly enough that afternoon, but as the leading units emerged from the south of the village they came under fire from an 88-mm gun deployed to their west in the Zonsche Forest. A team was despatched to deal with the gun and the push towards the bridge continued in earnest, but when the main group were within just 50 yd from the canal, an explosion destroyed the bridge and with it any chance that XXX Corps had of a swift advance towards Nijmegen. The destruction of the crossing also thwarted the swift movement of the 506th south to Eindhoven, a place that they were to have reached late that afternoon, and before the regiment could advance south in any numbers, a footbridge had to be constructed across the Wilhelmina canal. This crossing point, made of wood supplied by the inhabitants of Son, was not finished until midnight and by that time Sink had decided that it was prudent not to order his men into Eindhoven in the dark. Sink's decision not to advance was well founded: the city was not his primary objective; he wanted to keep as many men as possible alive for the fighting that he anticipated would be intense in the coming days, and he lacked communication with XXX Corps due to the non-arrival of crucial signals personnel. Had Sink been able to ascertain accurately XXX Corp's situation, his decision not to tackle Eindhoven that night would have undoubtedly been made far easier, but as was becoming a common feature of the operation, the ability for commanders to pass information to one another was not always what it should have been.

Having dropped on the northern portion of the main divisional DZ just to the south of St Oedenrode, Col John H. Michaelis's 502nd Parachute Infantry quickly moved off towards their objectives. A little later a patrol successfully made contact with the 501st at Veghel, while another company advanced south-west towards the bridge at Best. The capture of this crossing was planned to provide XXX Corps with an alternative route over the Wilhelmina canal if the Son bridge had been destroyed. In the circumstances, with the Son bridge destroyed, this option could have proved extremely useful, but it first had to be captured intact. 'H' Company emerged from the Zonsche Forest some 3 miles to the east of Son, but as it got within sight of the bridge, it ran into the defensive outposts of the German 59th Division. Attempts were made to circumvent the German positions and press home the attack to prevent the destruction of the crossing, but casualties were sustained and the defenders retained their cohesion. A platoon did manage to crawl forward to within a few hundred yards of the bridge, but they too could progress no further and the offensive lost the remainder of what little momentum it had left. As darkness fell it was decided that another attempt would be made on the bridge the next morning, and in preparation for this, the rest of the battalion, commanded by Lt Col Robert G. Cole, moved from the relative safety of Son to reinforce them.

By this time Veghel, 9 miles to the north-west, was safely in the hands of the 501st Parachute Infantry, but the day had not been without incident for Col Howard R. Johnson's men. The battalion that was meant to have dropped just to the north-west of Veghel had been incorrectly dropped some 4½ miles further to the west. This error meant that while its two accurately inserted sister battalions were in a position to attack their objectives immediately, Lt Col Kinnard's men had a long march before they were in a position to do the same. In the end, the time delay did not result in too many difficulties for the regiment, as its more southerly battalions managed to capture the village of Eerde successfully, block the road between Veghel and St Oedenrode, and capture both the railway and road bridges over the Zuid Willems canal and the road bridge over the Aa, while Kinnard's men took the railway bridge over the same river without a fight. Nevertheless, by the early evening a threat to these newly acquired objectives was building up in the west, for having left an outpost consisting of an officer and forty-six men at a large chateau adjacent to their DZ, Kinnard received word that they were under attack. A platoon was sent back to the chateau that night to reinforce the position but by morning a patrol reported that the position, had been overrun and only the detritus of battle remained.

The mixed results of the 101st Airborne Division on Sunday 17 September accurately reflected the rather patchy success of the other two airborne divisions and XXX Corps on that same day. A number of crucial bridges had been successfully seized, but Arnhem bridge had the equivalent of only a single battalion defending one end, the Nijmegen bridges were still in German hands, and the bridge at Son had been destroyed. The fact that the Wilhelmina canal could not be crossed in the short-term might have caused the Guards Armoured Division more immediate difficulties had they actually reached Eindhoven that evening as planned. Instead, tired after their struggle up the single road towards the city, the XXX Corps spearhead halted in Valkenswaard 10 miles from the bridge and busied themselves with preparations for an advance that would continue on the following day. As a consequence, crucial XXX Corps bridging materials remained some considerable distance from where they were required that night and the Germans, already recovering from the initial shock of the offensive and moving units to key locations, were able to take maximum advantages of the flaws in the Allied plan. The decisions that had been taken by various people not to fly a double lift on the first day, not to strike out more forcefully towards the Nijmegen bridges and not to drop parachutists closer to the Arnhem bridge, were all deficiencies that the Germans were able to capitalise on from the outset. Nevertheless, the 18th promised the arrival of even more airborne troops and guns in Holland and a renewed punch by XXX Corps. The situation was not yet critical, but much depended upon the strength of the German riposte.

THREE

18–19 SEPTEMBER – BREAKING THROUGH

The night of the 17/18 September was a busy one for John Frost at Arnhem bridge as his small forced organised their defences in twenty-five buildings. From the 250-yd wide base, the perimeter ballooned slightly to 375 yd at its widest point and was about 270 yd from top to bottom. At dawn, with precious little time for any rest, Frost's men with two 3-in mortars and six 6-pounder anti-tank guns, were in position and anxiously awaiting whatever the daylight hours brought – and at this stage in the operation they knew for certain that it was not going to be the advanced guard of XXX Corps. Frost's understandable feeling of isolation was exacerbated by his part in the widespread 1st Airborne Division communication failure. It could have been worse, however, for although the sets of the parachute units at the bridge were unable to make contact with anybody else, the Forward Observation Officer (FOO) of the 1st Light Regiment RA who was with them was able to contact his 75mm guns positioned near Oosterbeek church. Having attained radio contact during the night after a brave dash back to the Royal Artillery headquarters in Wolfheze to reset his radio and collect more batteries, the FOO provided a link to Oosterbeek which was maintained throughout the battle in Arnhem. It is interesting to note that the artillery had the same twenty-two sets as the parachute units, but the gunners managed to get them to work.

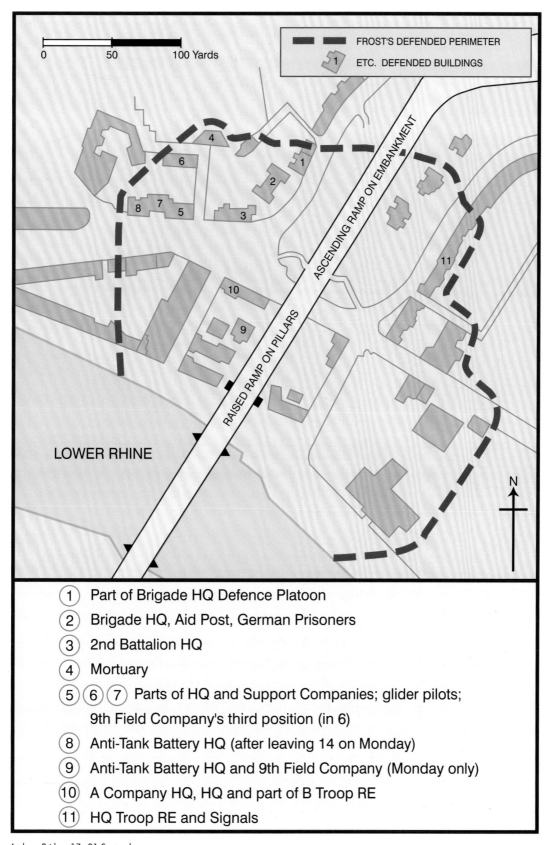

Legend on map:

FROST'S DEFENDED PERIMETER
1 ETC. DEFENDED BUILDINGS

0   50   100 Yards

ASCENDING RAMP ON EMBANKMENT

RAISED RAMP ON PILLARS

LOWER RHINE

N

(1) Part of Brigade HQ Defence Platoon
(2) Brigade HQ, Aid Post, German Prisoners
(3) 2nd Battalion HQ
(4) Mortuary
(5)(6)(7) Parts of HQ and Support Companies; glider pilots;
     9th Field Company's third position (in 6)
(8) Anti-Tank Battery HQ (after leaving 14 on Monday)
(9) Anti-Tank Battery HQ and 9th Field Company (Monday only)
(10) A Company HQ, HQ and part of B Troop RE
(11) HQ Troop RE and Signals

Arnhem Bridge, 17–21 September.

The Arnhem road bridge on the morning of 18 September with the lower part of Frost's defensive perimeter clearly visible. Several of the buildings to the right of the northern ramp were held at this time by a mixture of airborne units including 2Para, 3Para and sappers. To the left of the ramp, men of 2Para and some sappers held several of the buildings closest to the bridge. *(IWM MH.2061)*

The first action in Arnhem on the 18th came when some German troops pulled up in trucks close to the 2Para headquarters, apparently not knowing that they were in immediate danger. The firefight that ensued quickly escalated into a much larger action as colleagues began to probe the perimeter from the east using tanks and infantry. A little later that morning a number of German armoured cars attempted to drive across the bridge from its southern end. These troops were men from the 9th SS Panzer Division's Reconnaissance Battalion which had managed to cross the bridge the previous evening en route for Nijmegen, but come the morning and their attempt to return, they found their route back into Arnhem blocked. The first four reconnaissance vehicles caught the airborne defenders quite by surprise and raced across the bridge where they reached safety. The next vehicles, however, were stopped by a combination of PIATs, anti-tanks guns and some of Capt Eric Mackay's sappers dropping grenades from their buildings on the east side of the bridge into the open-topped half-tracks. Around twenty German vehicles were destroyed in this action which lasted a couple of hours. Frost's capture of the northern end of the bridge gave the Germans all sorts of problems as they endeavoured to deploy troops to counter the airborne landings. The 10th SS Panzer Division, for example, had been ordered to Nijmegen on the previous afternoon in order to safeguard the crossings over the Waal, but because of 2Para's success, subsequently needed to find an alternative place to cross the Lower Rhine so as to get to the city. The crossing point that they chose was at Pannerden, 6 miles to the south-east of

The northern end of Arnhem bridge during the battle, taken on 18 September from a Spitfire, showing the wreckage that resulted from an attempt by 9th SS Panzer Division's Reconnaissance Battalion to charge across the bridge from its southern end. The Lower Rhine is just out of shot on the right. (IWM MH.2062)

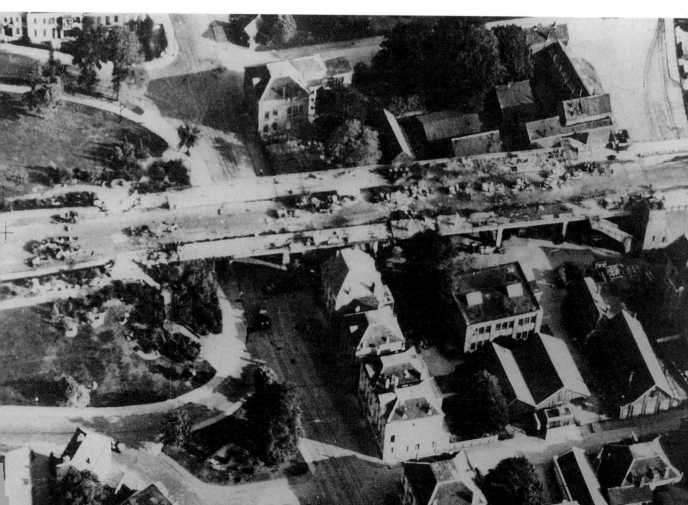

Arnhem, but there was no bridge and the situation was far from ideal. The trucks would cross the river by ferry first and later, when their engineers had built a bridge, the armour and heavier vehicles would follow. This complicated means of attaining a link to the south bank of the Lower Rhine inevitably meant it would take the division far longer to reach Nijmegen, especially as Allied air superiority posed such a threat that the bridge could only be built at

The road on which the Germans deployed, thus forcing Urquhart to remain in the attic of a house approximately halfway down the first row on the left. At the end of the road is the railway line and, out of shot just to the right, is St Elizabeth's hospital. *(Author's Collection)*

The house near St Elizabeth's hospital where General Urquhart took refuge during 18/19 September. *(Author's Collection)*

night, and would have to deploy a little at a time. However, some infantry from the 10th SS Panzer Division did manage to get through to Nijmegen by the morning of the 18th, immediately relieving elements of its sister division's reconnaissance battalion. But they then ran into Frost's positions at the bridge, as has been seen, and suffered heavy losses. These unfortunate German troops were returning to Arnhem to rejoin their parent unit when they ran the gauntlet through the pre-surveyed killing zone of the British units.

British paratroopers settling down in their C-47 having just emplaned. The rather large-looking grinning soldier on the right had obviously decided to take no chances on his jump as his rifle has been carefully covered to protect it, and he has chosen to wear a rather unflattering stole which was worn over his smock and webbing in order to prevent equipment snagging when his parachute deployed. *(IWM K.7586)*

Airlanding troops at the Wolfheze crossroads. The man lying prone is armed with a Projector Infantry Anti-Tank (PIAT), a weapon of very short range which was mounted on a bi-pod and fired an armour-piercing finned bomb. These weapons were held at section level and were extremely important to airborne forces that could boast little in the way of protective firepower. *(IWM BU.1144)*

The 9th SS Panzer Division had an important job to do. After its Kampfgruppe Brinkmann had retaken the north end of Arnhem bridge, it was to push west, link up Kampfgruppe Spindler, which had moved into blocking positions towards Oosterbeek, and von Tettau's force approaching from the west, and destroy the British airborne division.

Brinkmann put the defences at Arnhem bridge under considerable pressure during the afternoon of the 18th by employing mortars, infantry, armoured cars and SP guns, but his firepower and probing failed to shrink the perimeter despite managing to set many buildings on fire. Throughout that time excellent supporting work was done by the British guns in Oosterbeek (controlled by the FOO at Arnhem bridge), which laid down accurate fire and fragmented numerous German attacks. Nevertheless, just one day into the battle and the airborne forces in Arnhem had already been forced to dig deep into their reserves of stamina and their limited resources. Frost, moreover, was also concerned that he had received no word on the progress of XXX Corps, had only scant information about the situation in Oosterbeek, and that some of the prisoners that his men had taken, rather than being the scratch troops that he had expected, were the men of an elite SS Panzer division.

Meanwhile, while Brinkmann and Frost grappled with each other at the bridge, Kampfgruppe Spindler established a blocking line along the Dreijenseweg and south through to Oosterbeek, to thwart any British attempts to strengthen Frost at the bridge. The first of Spindler's units had, in fact, already engaged the advancing

DZ 'Y' looking south from the Amsterdamseweg. *(Author's Collection)*

Brig P.H.W. Hicks, commander of the 1st Airlanding Brigade, on 18 September. Hicks and Brig Hackett had stern words with each other after 4th Parachute Brigade landed on 18 September, as Hicks had taken over command of the division in Urquhart's absence and Hackett was not happy with the situation. *(IWM BU.1152)*

parachutists during the previous evening and they
had then been joined by Krafft's troops as they
withdrew towards Arnhem after their important
defensive work against 1st Parachute Brigade. 1
and 3Para struggled forward towards their
objectives against these well organised German
troops on the morning of the 18th. Having
encountered opposition on Tiger route during the
previous evening, 3Para moved south on to 2Para's
Lion route at around 0430 hr on the morning of
the 18th in an attempt to outflank the enemy.
Accompanied by both Lathbury and Urquhart, the
battalion fragmented as it attempted this difficult
manoeuvre in the darkness just before dawn, but
struggled on in an attempt to maintain their
momentum. 3Para were followed on to Lion route
by 1Para, which had pushed to their south-east
after running into the enemy on the previous
afternoon and during the night had moved through
the woods towards Johannahoeve, the railway line,
Oosterbeek and thence on to Tiger route by the
river. As both battalions dropped down from their
planned routes, they were constantly harassed by
the enemy and took some heavy casualties. Having
been forced south to the river, both battalions were
hemmed in and forced, if they were to reach
Arnhem bridge, to attack in an area densely packed
with buildings, through the bottleneck of Den Brink
and then on to St Elizabeth's hospital. Here, the
Germans waited for the inevitable British attack, for
it was an ideal place to sap the airborne offensive
strength and, furthermore, to deliver the final blow
to any chance that the division had of reaching
Arnhem bridge.

The lead elements of 3Para managed to fight
their way through to the imposing St Elizabeth's

hospital, but by that stage their numbers had dwindled alarmingly and they were too weak to punch a hole through a well-situated defensive position consisting of infantry, tanks and armoured cars. 1Para followed on behind, but even with this extra added power, the British could not crack open the enemy's defences and the fighting became intense, bloody and confused. By dusk both battalions had been drastically reduced in number with 3Para fighting with only 100 men in the vicinity of the hospital and, situated just to their east, 1Para struggling to make sense of the battle and desperately trying to do something to retrieve the situation. Sandwiched between them were German infantry and numerous vehicles. It was at this time that Urquhart's small party came under fire and Lathbury was wounded and had to be dragged into a nearby terraced house. Having shot a German through the open front door of the house with his revolver, certainly unusual for the commander of a division, Urquhart was forced to flee, but only made a few yards down an alley before having to take refuge in another house. The whole area was swarming with Germans, the airborne attacks in the vicinity did not seem to be making much headway and, stuck in an attic, Urquhart was unable to do anything about it. He consoled himself, however, with the knowledge that having seen transport aircraft arrive over to the west, that the

Men of the 2/South Staffordshire Regiment who arrived with the second lift, moving into Oosterbeek along the Utrechtseweg on 18 September. As troops travelled as light as possible, heavy items of kit and equipment were carried in jeeps. This jeep is towing an extremely valuable 6-pounder anti-tank gun. *(IWM BU 1091)*

German army and airforce personnel taken prisoner by American airborne forces in the vicinity of Nijmegen. The airforce troops are wearing a flight blouse that was designed for ease of movement in the cockpit, but was so popular that it was worn by all ranks no matter what their job. *(IWM B.10170)*

second lift had arrived and these newly arrived men of the 4th Parachute Brigade, together with the released Airlanding Brigade, could give a useful boost to an attempt to break through the German line during the next day.

The 1st Airborne Division's second lift was delayed by the low cloud that smothered the airfields back in England on the morning of the 18th, but by the early afternoon weather conditions had improved and the transporters and gliders were able to take off. The crossing of the English Channel was uneventful, but the armada encountered considerably more flak than the first lift as they approached Holland and around ninety enemy fighters also tried to make their presence felt. Quite clearly, with the element of surprise having been lost, the Germans were in a better position to do all that they could to thwart Allied plans. However, weapons of war are only as good as the damage that they inflict, and the German flak caused little damage to the Allied aircraft; the Luftwaffe threat was dealt with in a clinical fashion by the Allied fighter escort. On DZ 'Y' at Ginkel Heath, an area protected by the King's Own Scottish Borderers and a platoon of the Pathfinders, all three battalions of Hackett's 4th Parachute Brigade dropped in tight formation. The first men of 10, 11 and 156Para to touch down did so at 1500 hr under sporadic German fire, but casualties were light and the lift was a great success. The gliders also landed safely on two LZs, 204 of the wooden aircraft on LZ 'X' (which had been DZ 'X' for the first lift) north of Heelsum, and 69 on LZ 'S' to the north of Wolfheze. These gliders contained the balance of the 1st Airlanding Brigade and divisional troops. A total of 4,000 men landed in the second lift that afternoon and they had the potential to make a great difference to the division's fortunes, but they were not helped by the fact that they were late into battle and had precious little time to influence the course of events on the 18th before the light failed.

Nevertheless, attempts were made to push on towards Arnhem that evening, but it did not take long for them to run into the waiting Germans. Taking a route along the northern side of the railway line into the city, at 2000 hr, 156Para ran into Spindler's blocking line along the Dreijenseweg. As they approached the road the paratroopers went to ground as soon as German small arms fire clattered into them from unseen positions. Lt Col Sir Richard de Voeux, their commanding officer, wisely decided to disengage and to withdraw a mile or so in order that a deliberate attack could be organised. Once again, with their great asset of speed and surprise stripped away from them, the lightly armed airborne forces suffered as they advanced into contact with a waiting enemy, which had had many hours to prepare its defences. This situation was certainly not helped by the command, control and communications problems that the division was suffering from. With the radios not working and Urquhart and Lathbury still 'missing', command of the division had reverted to Brig Hicks that morning. Urquhart had mentioned that this would be the case to his chief of staff, Lt Col Charles Mackenzie, but he had neglected to tell 'Shan' Hackett, his senior brigadier, the same. On 18th the divisional headquarters moved forward to the Hartenstein Hotel and from here Hicks issued an order that as soon as the 4th Parachute Brigade landed that afternoon, one battalion, 11Para, would be taken from it and be used in an attempt to break through to Frost at the bridge. Hicks based his decision on the necessity to reinforce Frost as soon as possible as he was receiving word via the Royal Artillery net that the intensity of the German attacks at the bridge was increasing.

Doing what he could to increase the quantity of troops trying to push through into Arnhem, Hicks had already released a portion of the 2nd Battalion South Staffordshire Regiment from their job of defending LZ 'S' for the second lift so that they might reinforce 1 and 3Para. These men left their positions at 1030 hr that morning and reached the area of Den Brink early in the afternoon before themselves coming under some heavy fire. As soon as Hackett's brigade landed Hicks despatched the newly arrived 11Para, together with the remainder of the South Staffordshires, to push forward towards the St Elizabeth's. Hackett was far from happy about the

Overleaf: The population of Eindhoven, the first Dutch city to be liberated, celebrate by gathering in the streets and dancing. The look of concern on the faces of some, however, might be due to the fact that fighting could still be heard just to the north as the US 101st Airborne Division fended off German counter-attacks around Son. *(IWM B.10125)*

command situation when he landed, but he was angry that he had been ordered to release a third of his total force without any kind of consultation, especially as it involved sending his men into the fray as darkness descended. 11Para stood patiently by waiting for their orders as the two brigadiers sorted out their differences. The discussions were heated and again highlighted the many problems caused by Urquhart's decision to move away from his headquarters on the 17th and his failure to fully inform his brigadiers about who would take over the command of the division in his absence. Nevertheless, the two men did come to a compromise over their problem and new orders were issued to the effect that just before dawn on the 19th 11Para would advance via the river road, as Hicks had wanted, in an attempt to link up with 1 and 3Para, while the rest of 4th Parachute Brigade, with the 7th Battalion of the King's Own Scottish Borderers under command, would attack the German defensive line along the Dreijenseweg. These attacks, it was argued, would provide the best chance for a link up with Frost's men in Arnhem and meant that for the time being, the British retained the initiative and took the battle to the enemy. Just one day into the battle and staff officers at the Hartenstein were already concerned that when XXX Corps reached Arnhem bridge, there would be no airborne soldiers there to greet them, only the massed guns, tanks and infantry of an SS Panzer Division.

In order for the Guards Armoured Division to press on to Arnhem as soon as they could after reaching Nijmegen, it was important for the 82nd Airborne Division to have taken at least one of the two crossings that they required over the Waal. Attempts to do so began at 0745 hr on 18 September when men of the 508th attacked towards the road bridge. Approaching from the south-east, the Americans came under fire simultaneously from German artillery on the north bank of the river and a mixture of weapons deployed in a strong defensive position, which incorporated the Hunner Park and a medieval observation tower called the Belvedere, at the southern end of the bridge. The parachutists managed to advance to a roundabout approximately 200 yd from the bridge, but such was the ferocity of the German defence that they could go no further.

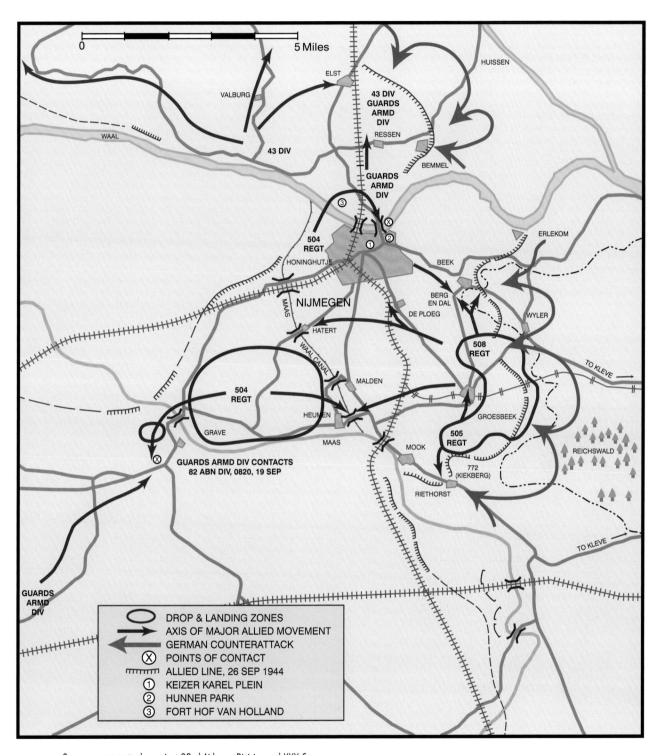

German counter-attacks against 82nd Airborne Division and XXX Corps.

A CG-4A glider crew awaits its compliment of US 101st Airborne Division soldiers before taking off for [...] and as part of the second lift. (ASOME)

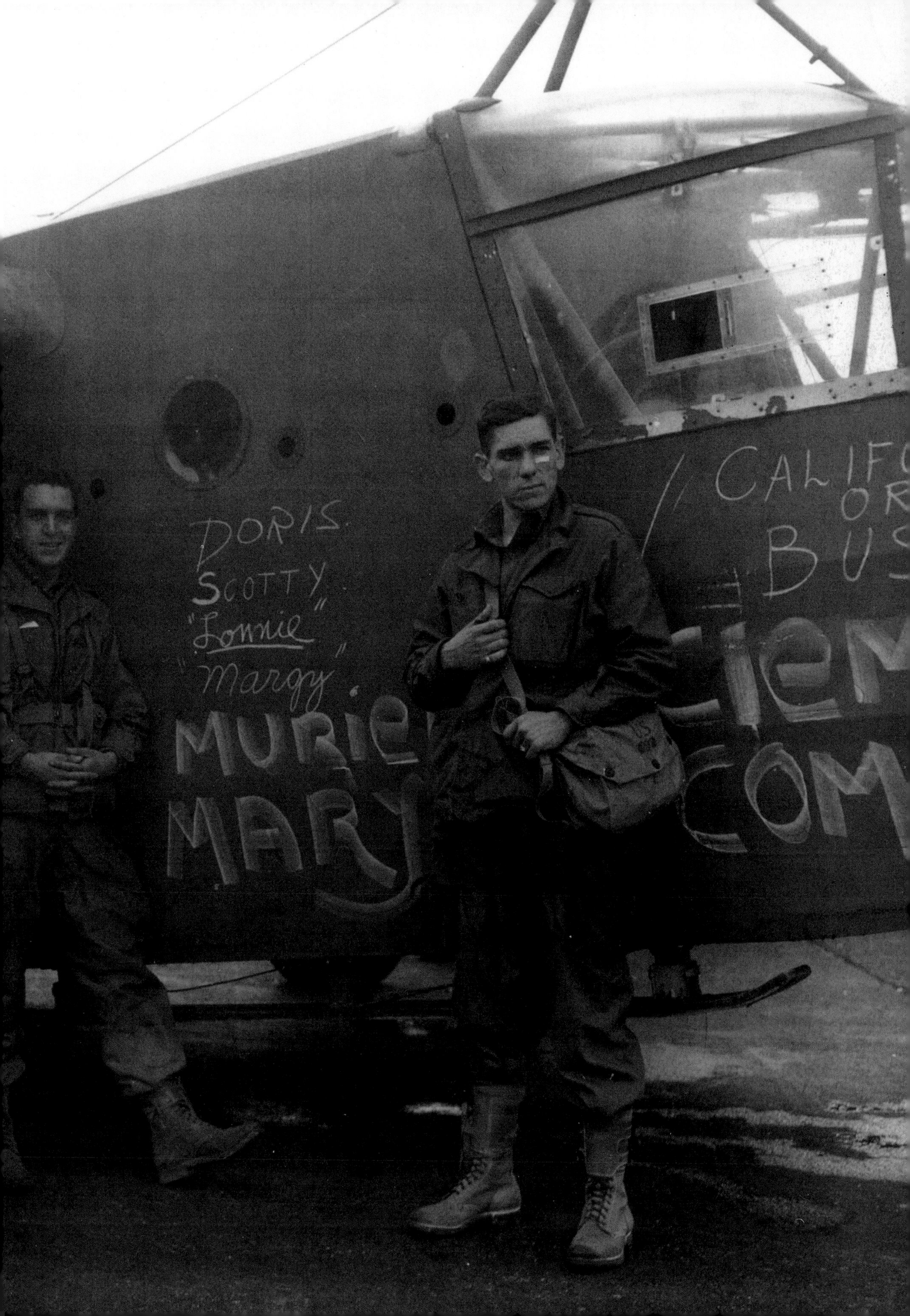
DORIS
SCOTTY
"Lonnie"
"Margy"

The lack of appropriate heavy weaponry to deal with a situation such as this was a common problem for all airborne forces, but this disadvantage was exaggerated by the fact that the attacking Americans were so few in number. Indeed, 82nd Airborne Division had so few resources to devote to the taking of the bridges over the Waal that their attempts might be considered doomed from the outset. To make matters worse, while the 508th were attacking in Nijmegen, Gavin's thinly stretched division was put under intense pressure when the Germans launched attacks on the American LZs that were required for their second lift. Although these probes were eventually rebuffed by the division, Gavin was so fearful that the enemy might succeed in overrunning their positions that he ordered the attack on Nijmegen bridge to be stopped and the troops there to be redeployed in defence of his most northerly LZ. The men of the 1st Battalion of the 508th marched the 8 miles from Nijmegen to the LZ and arrived there just in time to stop the Germans from marauding over the area. In a sense, it was fortuitous that the second lift into Holland was delayed in England, for by the time that they arrived that afternoon the LZ, which had been under great pressure that morning, had been successfully secured – albeit only just in some areas. That afternoon 450 gliders landed safely in the 82nd Airborne divisional area and the 1,800 men, 8 anti-tank guns, 36 field howitzers, 200 jeeps and 120 trailers provided a welcome boost to Gavin's assets – especially as he had received news from the Dutch underground that despite what had been thought on the previous day, German armour was massing in the Reichswald. Despite this new threat, as soon as the second lift touched down Browning told Gavin to prepare a plan to capture the two bridges in Nijmegen. The corps commander's priorities had shifted slightly and the Waal crossings were to be taken, not at the expense of the Germans swarming over the divisional sector, but with some haste, for XXX Corps were timetabled to arrive in the area that evening.

Elsewhere in Gavin's sector his troops spent the day strengthening their positions and preparing for the arrival of the Guards. During this period, for example, the 508th secured Beek and the larger part of the 504th established defences to protect the western approaches

American ground crew watch as Douglas C-47 Dakotas fly over their airfield while yet more aircraft wait on the ground. The C-47 was the stalwart of the US Troop Carrier Command and was operated by a four-man crew: two pilots, a wireless operator and a navigator. *(IWM EA.37863)*

to Nijmegen against a German assault. Meanwhile, elements of the 508th and the 504th struck out for the Honinghutje bridge over the Maas-Waal canal, the preferred crossing point for XXX Corps as it was on the most direct route into Nijmegen. The two units made good progress and saw little sign of the enemy as they approached the bridge. As they moved forward, however, there was an explosion, the parachutists hit the ground and in an instant the bridge had been rendered impassable to heavy vehicles. It was as a result of the destruction of the span at Honinghutje that the bridge at Heumen, the only crossing over the canal taken intact, became so important, despite it necessitating a more circuitous route to the Waal.

Men of the US 101st Airborne Division explore the wreckage of one of their gliders on 18 September. It did not take more than a slight miscalculation by a pilot for the nose of glider to dig into the soft Dutch soil and for the whole aircraft to flip over and break up. *(IWM EA.38134)*

The bridge at Son looking north-west. It was destroyed by the Germans as troops from 101st Airborne Division advanced towards it up the road from the right. *(Author's Collection)*

As a result it had to be protected and partly to ensure its security, but also to shore up the southerly portion of the divisional sector, the 505th captured key villages in the vicinity, such as Mook, and a buffer zone was created around the crossing.

By the evening Gavin had devised his plan for the taking of the Nijmegen road bridge and it required a battalion of the 504th, in conjunction with a battalion of the 508th, to envelop the bridge that night. Browning, however, was not particularly happy with this idea, for he was concerned that the redeployment of so many troops would render the high ground and the Heumen bridge vulnerable to any sustained German action emanating from the east and specifically, the Reichswald. Indeed, the threat to the high ground grew so much that afternoon that Gavin had be forced to call on nearly 100 fighter aircraft of the British Second Tactical Air Force to bomb and strafe the forest in an attempt to relieve some of the

St Elizabeth's hospital. The scene of much fighting just outside its front door while life-saving work was being carried out by surgical teams inside. *(Author's Collection)*

1 Para got this close to Arnhem bridge. This picture was taken from the top of the steep bank separating the Utrechtseweg and the river road just by St Elizabeth's hospital. *(Author's Collection)*

A supply basket drops on the Utrechtseweg just outside the Hartenstein Hotel on 19 September. As the defensive perimeter formed around the hotel, it became increasingly difficult for the airborne troops to recover any of the supplies dropped to them by the RAF. *(IWM BU.1093)*

pressure on his defending troops. The net result of the German attacks on the high ground was that the Gavin's plans for an attack in Nijmegen were postponed, thus revealing that Browning still believed that the Groesbeek Heights needed to be secure before a Waal crossing should be taken. This was a decision based on sound reasoning, but seems at odds with the need for XXX Corps to advance quickly, the parlous situation of the Market Garden at that time, and, as already mentioned, the lack of any view into Nijmegen from certain positions that Browning believed would be crucial enemy observation points. Clearly Browning's decision was one of great gravity, for without a crossing point XXX Corps would inevitably be delayed and the attainment of 'the prize', a crossing over the Lower Rhine at Arnhem, would be in even greater doubt.

The difficulties that Urquhart's division had were not known about in any great detail by Gavin and Browning due to the communications problem, but the little information that did get through to them underlined the need for XXX Corps to get there as quickly as possible. On the morning of the 18th, for example, a message got through to the 505th by a civilian telephone line from the Dutch Resistance which reported 'Germans winning over British at Arnhem'. Even so, by that evening plans to seize a Waal crossing had been shelved and the main elements of Horrocks's corps were still two and a half hours away from linking up with the 101st Airborne Division in Eindhoven.

The advance of the Irish Guards at the tip of XXX Corps's spearhead began from Valkenswaard at 0600 hr on 18 September. The need for the Guards Armoured Division to get some momentum into their attack was obvious, but at the village of Aalst after little more than a mile had been covered, they were delayed by a solitary SP gun which slammed its rounds into the lead tanks. This set the tone for the morning, a continuation of the problems that the attacking units had experienced on the previous day, isolated pockets of German resistance taking an inordinate amount of time to clear before the advance could continue. All attempts to outflank the enemy positions were thwarted by the soft ground, narrow roads, weak bridges either side of the main road, and the woods and houses adjacent to their main axis which provided ample cover for the waiting Germans. Close air support would certainly have aided the armour at this stage, but there was none to be had as the Typhoons were grounded by fog at their Belgian airfields although, annoyingly for Adair, the skies over Holland were clear. It would also have been of great advantage to the operation had the British been able to put the Germans under pressure on a front wider than just one single road, but the formations on the flanks of XXX Corps, VIII on the right and XII Corps on the left, only broke the enemy defences on the Meuse-Escaut canal during the of the night 18th. Thus, by late morning the Guards Armoured Division was fighting hard up the road to Eindhoven, but was still several miles short of the city. A few hours later a couple of British armoured cars

The steep bank separating the lower river road from the Utrechtseweg just by St Elizabeth's hospital. *(Author's Collection)*

from the Household Cavalry did manage to outflank the enemy, speed into Eindhoven and link up with the newly arrived 506th from 101st Airborne Division, but the situation was far from satisfactory.

The 506th had set off for their objective at 0600 hr after crossing the Wilhelmina canal over a temporary footbridge the night before. As they moved cautiously towards Eindhoven they did run into some Germans, but they were not delayed for long by them and they entered the city in late morning somewhat surprised by the lack of a strong enemy presence. By midday the regiment had taken four bridges in the area and then proceeded to consolidate their position while awaiting the arrival of XXX Corps. By this time the local Dutch people were celebrating their liberation and were clogging the streets in their joy. Thus, when the lead tanks of the Irish Guards did enter the city at 1900 hr anxious to get to Son as quickly as possible, they were immediately slowed to a crawl. Nevertheless, conscious

The museum near St Elizabeth's hospital where the Germans had a blocking position which thwarted attempts to break through to Arnhem bridge on the morning of 19 September. *(Author's Collection)*

that they should have been approaching Nijmegen by this stage, the armour pushed on to the Wilhelmina canal in the growing darkness and when they got there XXX Corps engineers immediately set about throwing a Bailey bridge across the water obstacle.

Meanwhile, the rest of the 101st Airborne Division busied itself in repelling German probes towards their positions or were preparing to do so. There had been a German counter-attack on Veghel during the night, but this, together with other forays by the enemy, had largely been information-gathering ventures and did not at this time pose a great threat to the security of the airborne division. Even so, at Best, the alternative crossing point of the Wilhelmina canal, the Americans did struggle to get to the bridge as the Germans were well aware of the importance of the crossing to the Allies. As a result, the fighting here on the 18th was intense and both sides poured more resources into the area. During this time the small and isolated party of parachutists lying low close to the bridge could do little more than wait to be reinforced as the battle raged around them. The Germans meanwhile, cleverly sucked the already stretched airborne troops towards them having secretly destroyed the bridge at 1100 hr that morning. The German counter-attacks that followed during the afternoon put greater pressure on the 502nd, for any loss of ground in the area prejudiced the eagerly anticipated bridging of the canal and it was crucial that this should take place unmolested. The situation at Best remained in the balance that afternoon, but the tenacious Americans skilfully held on to their position in the Zonsche Forest aided by the timely arrival of some Typhoons providing close air support, and a British armoured car and a reconnaissance car which appeared on the south bank and remained there until the evening.

The 101st Airborne Division was stretched by German actions all over their sector on the morning of the 18th and it was, therefore, a great comfort to Taylor when he saw the aircraft of the second lift approaching that afternoon. This lift, in common with those of the other two airborne divisions on that day, was delayed by fog, but unlike the others it was of more mixed success. That afternoon, although two battalions of the 327th Glider Infantry, some divisional troops, artillery, jeeps and trailers were all accurately delivered, 50 per cent of their valuable resupply drop went awry. In spite of this, these troops certainly strengthened Taylor's situation and by the end of the day the division was in a relatively comfortable position, but was concerned by the late arrival of XXX Corps. Their concerns were well-founded for while the Guards Armoured Division waited for a crossing at Son to be completed that evening they should, according to Horrocks's estimations, have been in Nijmegen readying themselves to cross the Waal. The fact that Operation Garden was so far behind schedule and German resistance to the thrust was so much more formidable than had been anticipated, meant that the success of Operation Market Garden was, at the end of the second day, already in the balance. To restore the situation the Guards Armoured Division needed to put on a burst of speed that would take them to the southern end of Arnhem bridge within twenty-four hours. The likelihood of this happening, however, was slim, for the German counter-attacks along the corridor were strengthening, the Nijmegen crossings were still firmly in enemy hands and the weather forecast in England for the third lift on the following day was poor.

By the morning of 19 September, the British situation at Arnhem bridge was serious, but defeat and surrender were not seen as options for its defenders. With the men under Frost's command still enjoying high morale and having inflicted some severe casualties on the enemy, they were sure that despite their lack of information, they would see XXX Corps rolling across the bridge at any time. To give the advancing armour the best possible chance of getting to the Lower Rhine, the airborne troops at the bridge understood that they had to hold on to their position for as long as possible despite the pressure that they were under. Some bold German attacks, especially on the eastern side of the perimeter, involved the use of armoured cars, but although these were stopped by 6-pounder anti-tank guns, ammunition was beginning to get alarmingly short and there was the potential for an enemy breakthrough if their commanders concentrated their resources on one spot. The British stand in Arnhem became remarkable for its tenacity and the professionalism

Oosterbeek church adjacent to the Lower Rhine where Maj Dickie Lonsdale addressed troops which had fallen back on this position on 20 September. It was in this area that the guns of Lt Col Thompson's Light Regiment were deployed. *(Author's Collection)*

of the men that were surrounded there. The fact that the attacking Germans paid so much respect to the men at the bridge was testament to the defenders' abilities and heroism, and was, perhaps, a major contributing factor in why Frost's dwindling group managed to hold out for so long.

Nevertheless, the German decision to grind the airborne soldiers down did begin to pay dividends on the 19th, for weak spots began to appear in the perimeter and under the cover of their armour, guns and mortars, the German infantry began to probe and infiltrate. On the eastern side, for example, buildings held by sappers were targeted and by dusk, out of fifty men, four were dead and a further twenty-four were wounded. The systematic demolition of the buildings in the area had a debilitating effect on the defenders, but it was catastrophic for the casualties who were sheltering in the cellars. With only two doctors and a handful of medical orderlies, no water, medical supplies running short and their shelter collapsing around them, conditions went from bad to worse. Tuesday 19 September was a turning point in the battle at Arnhem bridge, for it was on this day that the Germans made their superior numbers count and on which they unleashed unceasing violence on the increasingly fragile perimeter. However, the determination of Frost to see the job through to a successful conclusion was reflected in his refusal to respond to a German request for his men to surrender. The commanding officer of 2Para had been instrumental in forging the British airborne esprit de corps and establishing their fearsome reputation on the battlefield, he was not going to give up while his men still had the means with which to fight. Even so, Frost did wonder that evening whether relief was likely to reach him, either in the form of XXX Corps or other elements of the 1st Airborne Division, before his position was overwhelmed. The Germans were suffocating his force in an ever-decreasing pocket, and there was very little that he could do about it.

Relief from the rest of Urquhart's division was far less likely by the end of the 19th than it had been that morning. The attack in the area of St Elizabeth's hospital was organised by the commanding officers of 1Para, 11Para (which had reached the area the previous

Short Stirlings flying at an altitude of about 1,000 feet on a resupply mission north of Oosterbeek on 19 September. The smoke came from bursting flak rounds. It is unlikely that much of this drop was recovered by the British airborne troops as the Germans had overrun the DZ. (J. Falconer)

The Hartenstein — one time mess for Model's staff, then Gen Urquhart's headquarters and now a superb museum about the Battle of Arnhem. (Author's Collection)

night) and the South Staffordshires, and was executed at 0400 hr. In the vicinity of the hospital the river road and the Utrechtseweg converged very briefly before being separated again by a high and extremely steep embankment. The attack along the upper road was conducted by the South Staffordshires supported by 11Para, while 1Para advanced along the lower road. Soon after the attack along the river began, 1Para ran into the survivors of 3Para who had tried to push through to the bridge alone during the previous night but had failed to break through. Coming up against strong German opposition, both on the road and on the higher ground to their left, the attack foundered and then was halted. The South Staffordshires ran into similar problems as they tried to advance past the hospital and towards the museum. After two hours of intense fighting in a small area in which mobility was limited by the buildings and embankment, this attack was also halted. The crucial early morning attempt to breakthrough to Frost had failed, and casualties had been extremely high, but it did at least give Urquhart a chance to escape from his protracted confinement in the attic and dash back to his headquarters in a jeep. The general officer's journey to the Hartenstein Hotel was not without incident as snipers took shots at his vehicle as it sped through the battle debris back into Oosterbeek, but he escaped injury and to the amazement of staff officers in the building who thought that he was probably dead, immediately sent Col Hilary Barlow, the deputy commander of the 1st Airlanding Brigade, to take control of the amalgam of troops fighting near St Elizabeth's hospital. Barlow left Oosterbeek soon after, but he was killed somewhere en route and his body was never recovered. This was a great blow to the men in the remains of the battalions that he had been sent to direct as all four had lost their commanding officers in the fighting that morning, and although desperate for a controlling influence and a guiding hand, they never received one.

The British lost their attacking initiative in the Battle of Arnhem–Oosterbeek on the morning of 19 September and they never regained it. During the day, all over the fragmented battlefield, the Germans began to strike back with increasing venom as they augmented their men and resources. The difficulty by this time for the British was that, although Urquhart was back at his headquarters, so many officers and NCOs had become casualties that it was difficult for their units to keep their shape and organisation. The situation became so desperate for the men fighting in their dramatically weakened battalions near the hospital that they began to withdraw back towards Oosterbeek along the river road. These men, although extremely tired, were met a few hundred yards short of the old Oosterbeek church by Lt Col 'Sheriff' Thompson, commander of the Light Regiment Royal Artillery, and told to establish a blocking position there. This area was correctly appreciated by Thompson as crucial to the health of the division for it was here that his guns continued to support Frost at the bridge, and with access to the Lower Rhine, provided the division with the option to either reinforce or to evacuate across the river. Four hundred men were eventually organised into this defensive position

British reconnaissance vehicles, led by an AEC armoured car, speed onwards towards Grave having recently crossed the Bailey bridge at Son. The AEC was armed with a 6-pounder gun and was the only British-built diesel-engined armoured car in service during the Second World War. *(IWM B.10147A)*

and known as 'Thompson Force', met the Germans that inevitably probed down the road later that afternoon. The fighting that took place there was at close quarters and was frenetic, but the line held, not least due to the actions of L Sgt John Baskeyfield of the South Staffordshires who won a posthumous Victoria Cross for fending off several German tanks with a 6-pounder anti-tank gun, and the Germans were stopped from infiltrating between the base of the British position and the river.

The dismemberment of the four battalions that fought under Thompson on the river road, was a fate also awaiting the battalions of the 4th Parachute Brigade as they launched their attack that same morning. In this push, 156Para sought to take the high ground of Koepel, while 10Para moved to protect their left flank by securing the ground at the northern end of the Dreijenseweg. At first all went well and some ground was taken as 156Para moved up to the Dreijenseweg and linked up with the King's Own Scottish Borderers who were situated in the area of Johannahoeve. These 1st Airlanding Brigade troops were defending an LZ that had been designated for the arrival of part of the Polish Brigade which was planned to land there that afternoon in the third lift, but had become exposed due to the various German counter-attacks. However, as 156Para attacked across the Dreijenseweg and into the woods on the other side, they ran into stiff German opposition and suffered heavy casualties, particularly among their officers. On the left 10Para did manage to secure their objective, but their colleagues to their south were engaged by some withering machine gun fire and were then strafed by some German Bf109 fighters. It would have been difficult on this day for the British airborne troops to have believed that the Allies had air superiority, verging on air supremacy, indeed, a little later they watched helplessly as an Allied resupply mission was flown in and the aircraft were hit hard by German flak from the surrounding high ground. The aircrews, however, were focused on their mission and they bravely flew in at 1,000 ft and

Lt Gen Frederick Browning and Brig Gen James Gavin confer near Groesbeek just after XXX Corps had linked up with the US 82nd Airborne Division. *(IWM HU.72434)*

A C-47 plunges towards the ground, crashes and is engulfed by a ball of flame close to an American LZ during Market Garden. *(ASOMF)*

then, when they were about 1 mile beyond the Dreijenseweg, disgorged their wares over Supply DZ 'V' – and into enemy hands. One pilot, Flt Lt David Lord, was awarded a posthumous Victoria Cross for his selflessness during this drop, but unfortunately only a tiny percentage of the supplies that parachuted in that afternoon ever reached the tired hands of the airborne troops.

It was clear to Urquhart by the early afternoon that the 4th Parachute Brigade's attack had failed and, furthermore, that it was dangerous for them to be separated any longer from the engorged divisional position based around his headquarters. However, between Hackett's men and the Hartenstein was a steep railway embankment that was passable by troops on foot, but not by jeeps and the valuable anti-tank guns. Three suitable crossing points across the embankment were quickly identified, and although the one at the southern end of the Dreijenseweg was in German hands, a tunnel near Wolfheze and the Wolfheze crossing itself were both held by the British. The 4th Parachute Brigade had to move quickly if it was not to be permanently divorced from the rest of the division in Oosterbeek, but just as it was making its preparations to move south, it received a message that the Wolfheze crossing was threatened by the enemy and that 10Para should immediately disengage and be sent to keep it open. This potentially dangerous redeployment of 10Para to Wolfheze was necessary, based on the information received about German attacks in the area, but in reality was not required as the situation there was not as desperate as had been thought. Nevertheless, as 10Para turned around and began to move south-east, they ran into Germans which had come in behind them, and were also followed by the enemy that they had pinned down during the morning. To make matters worse the Polish Brigade's gliders began to land as they crossed LZ 'L' and turned a difficult situation in a shambolic one. As the Poles worked to unload their jeeps and anti-tank guns, the whole area was raked by gun-fire, and trying to defend themselves in the confusion, opened fire on friendly forces as well as the enemy. The casualties that the Poles took during this period were bad enough, but their numbers would have been nothing to the men lost had a decision not been taken at

A British truck in the XXX Corps column burst into flames after being hit by a German shell. This wreck would have to be bulldozed off the road before it could be reopened to traffic. German guns could easily be secreted in any of the woods adjacent to the single road up which the British ground forces advanced, often slowly, towards Arnhem. *(IWM B.10124A)*

the last moment to cancel the drop of Sosabowski's three parachute battalions on the DZs south of Arnhem bridge which were still in enemy hands. In the event these units were withheld from the battle until a later date and were increasingly seen not as an anticipated consolidation force, but as vital reinforcements to bolster Urquhart's precarious position in Oosterbeek.

Both the King's Own Scottish Borderers and 156Para were unaware of this, however, as they disengaged from the enemy and withdrew 'without delay' towards Oosterbeek. As they did so, their enemy, sensing weakness, trailed the two battalions and waited for a good opportunity to destroy them. That opportunity seemed at hand for the Germans as these British battalions fragmented as they withdrew to a suitable crossing point or, indeed, clambered over the embankment itself under enemy fire, but they failed to take full advantage of it. As a result, when 10 and 156Para collected to the south of the railway embankment that night, although they amounted to just 250 and 176 officers and men respectively, they were still organised, well led and capable of further fighting. There had been many acts of bravery that night indeed, 10Para's Captain Lionel Quieripel, won a posthumous Victoria Cross during this phase of the battle, but the shattered remains of the withdrawing battalions still had to enter the defensive perimeter that was forming around the Hartenstein, and with the enemy all around them, that would not necessarily be easy.

The thumb-shaped perimeter that developed in Oosterbeek during the evening of 19 September consisted of an amalgam of units and included Thompson Force in its south-eastern corner. As darkness fell on the battlefield, elements of the 1st Airlanding Brigade were also already in situ, with the Border Regiment on the western side having taken up positions between the railway line and the high ground of Westerbouwing on the river. The Border Regiment had originally been detailed to defend the gains secured by the 1st Parachute Brigade in Arnhem, but the battle had not gone to plan and so they found themselves that evening defending an area several miles from the city. Alongside them on the western side of the perimeter were some glider pilots, the 21st Independent Parachute

C-47s carrying US 101st Airborne Division's second lift over liberated Belgian territory en route for Holland on 19 September. *(IWM B.10092)*

Company and the remains of the King's Own Scottish Borderers which had withdrawn through the Polish LZ, across the railway embankment and entered the perimeter at its northern end. In the east were more glider pilots, who were trained, unlike their American contemporaries, in an infantry role, Thompson Force and the Light Regiment RA. The development of the defensive position around the Hartenstein marked a new phase in the fighting, the Battle for the Oosterbeek Perimeter, but with 3,500 of the 5,500 men flown in already casualties and supplies of essentials, including ammunition, running short, time was not on Urquhart's side.

Infantry of the 231st Brigade of 50th Division crossing Joe's bridge and moving up in support of the Guards Armoured Division. *(IWM B.9981)*

That night, as the airborne troops tried to settle into their new positions around the divisional headquarters and Hackett prepared for his men to break into the perimeter, German armour and infantry swept around the northern side of the embankment while armoured cars and more infantry probed towards the positions held by 4th Parachute Brigade. The Germans had successfully squeezed the 1st Airborne Division into two shrinking pockets, one at Arnhem bridge and one in Oosterbeek, and from the evening of the 19th proceeded to destroy them. Pressing towards the Hartenstein from the north was Krafft, from the east was Spindler and from the west was von Tettau, each with a growing array of heavy weapons at their disposal. The Germans were strangling the 1st Airborne Division, and Urquhart knew it, but as they began to choke no saviour was yet in sight as the Germans continued to hold the bridges over the Waal.

The engineers finished building their Bailey bridge at Son shortly after dawn on 19 September, and at 0630 hr British armour started to move across it. The lead elements of the Guards Armoured Division, followed by the armoured cars of the Household Cavalry and the tanks and infantry of the Grenadier Guards, reached Veghel at around 0700 hr and Grave just 1 hour and 20 minutes later, but although good progress had been made that morning, these units were one and a half days behind schedule. Waiting for them were the 504th Parachute Infantry Regiment and Generals Browning and Gavin, who immediately conferred with senior officers and came up with a scheme to take the Waal crossings. The plan was for Browning's own regiment, the Grenadier Guards, to rush the two Nijmegen bridges with a battalion of the 505th under command. To further strengthen the 82nd Airborne Division against German attack from the east, it was also arranged for the Coldstream Guards Group of armour and infantry, to be attached to Gavin. The extra personnel, armour, anti-tank guns and artillery immediately took pressure off the division and allowed commanders to redeploy their forces. With the help from the Guards Armoured Division established, part of the 504th relieved a battalion of the 508th at Hatert, which was then sent to join the rest of its regiment at Berg en Dal. The arrival of XXX Corps in the 82nd Airborne Division's sector was timely, for not only had Gavin failed to receive his 325th Glider Infantry due to the bad weather, but German attacks were also developing in from the east. On the Groesbeek Heights, for example, Corps Feldt probed out of the Reichswald and towards American positions with the aim of destroying the airborne troops and recapturing the bridges over the Maas-Waal canal. Particularly stretched were the 508th at Berg en Dal and here important positions changed hands several times as the Germans pushed towards the eastern outskirts of Nijmegen. In such circumstances the parachutists fell back on their excellent training, camaraderie and experience, and although disadvantaged when 80 per cent of their resupply drop was lost due to scattering, they managed to hold on to their positions and safeguard operations in Nijmegen.

The attacks on the Nijmegen bridges did not actually start until mid-afternoon due to the extra time that it took the Guards Armoured Division to get to the city via Heumen bridge. The delays that had been incurred in the operation up to this point most obviously affected those airborne forces awaiting reinforcement by XXX Corps, but the fact that Operation Garden was so far behind schedule also had unhealthy ramifications for troops which became embroiled in hastily prepared attacks that sought to hasten the armoured advance. In Nijmegen, for example, little was known about the enemy's strength and deployments, especially around the railway bridge, and as a consequence the first push towards the Waal incorporating the Guards was something of an information-gathering exercise. Waiting for them were Bittrich's men, some from the 9th SS Panzer Division, but most from the 10th SS Panzer Division who, despite their own difficulties in crossing the Lower Rhine, had had enough time to reach Nijmegen and deploy before contacting Adair's men and machines. At 1500 hr the Grenadier Guards were guided to the railway bridge by local Dutch guides with American parachutists riding on five tanks and five armoured cars. When the lead elements were approximately 1,000 yd from the bridge, they were engaged by enemy fire, the infantry dismounted and they ran for the southern end of the crossing. These men, supported by the guns of their tanks, got to with 500 yd of their objective, but were then halted by small arms and a 20-mm gun and the lead tank was destroyed by an 88-mm round.

Meanwhile, an attack was launched against the road bridge from the east of the city taking the same route as the attempt on the previous day. This push also got to with a few hundred yards of its objective before being stopped by its German defenders. The fire power that the Germans brought to bear on the attacking Anglo-American force on this day was impressive, and by dusk, after a third attack had failed as it approached the road bridge, tanks, armoured cars and buildings were ablaze and corpses littered the streets. A vital crossing was not taken in Nijmegen on the 19th and Allied casualties had been substantial – already in the city hospital there were 600 American wounded and another 150 were missing or dead – but there was no thought of giving up with the 1st Airborne Division just a few miles up the road at Arnhem. Browning and Gavin met that evening to decide how to proceed. The result was a plan to take both ends of the two bridges simultaneously by transporting some American airborne troops across the Waal in boats and then launching attacks from both the north and the south. The possibility that the Germans would demolish the bridges as soon as the Allies set foot on them was a constant threat, but if that was what the enemy wanted to do then there was nothing that could be done to stop them. Bittrich had, in fact, urged for the demolition of the bridges at Arnhem and Nijmegen from the outset, but Model would not allow it, for (heavily influenced by Hitler) he was confident that the Allies could be stopped and believed that the crossings would be vital in the German counter-attacks that followed.

Gavin's plan was to relieve Tucker's 504th from their guard duties at Grave and to use them to cross the 400-yd wide Waal 1 mile downstream from the railway bridge. Supported as they crossed by the guns of the Guards Armoured Division, the parachutists were then to attack the northern end of the two bridges as renewed attempts were made to capture the southern ends. Thirty-three canvas assault craft were offered by Horrocks for the mission, but as the boats still had to be located in XXX Corp's column and then

The first prisoners taken by 158th Brigade of XII Corps's 53rd Division in Holland. These German parachutists put up stout resistance but were eventually overwhelmed on 19 September. *(IWM B.10096)*

moved up the narrow road to Nijmegen, it was decided that the attack could not take place until daylight on the 20th.

The XXX Corps traffic jam in which the assault craft were caught up stretched back way beyond the Meuse-Escaut canal and the flow of vehicles up the single road towards Nijmegen was only made more difficult by a German bombing raid on the night of 19/20 September. That evening around one hundred twin-engined aircraft caused widespread destruction in Eindhoven (and considerable British and Dutch casualties), so XXX Corps traffic was consequently held up for a day while the town was cleared. The new Son bridge was also targeted by the Germans who did all that they could to cause the Allies advance to falter. There was a great deal of action at Best during the 19th as the Germans tried to push into Son and, not knowing that the bridge had already been destroyed, the Americans tried to seize the crossing in counter-attacks. It was during one German attack that morning that PFC Joe E. Mann of 'H' Company 502nd, wounded four times on Monday, was killed in an isolated position near the bridge when he threw himself on a German grenade which threatened the lives of six other men. Mann was posthumously awarded the Congressional Medal of Honour for a battle that cost both sides many casualties and continued unabated until the mid-afternoon. The decisive moment, however, came at 1400 hr when two battalions of the 506th and some units of the 327th Glider Infantry Regiment, supported by British armour from the 15th/19th Hussars, attacked and finally destroyed the German ability to mount further sustained offensive action in the area. This was an important success for the Allies as a buffer zone was created between Best and the crucial Son crossing. But there was no time for complacency, for to the east the 107th Panzer Brigade and the 208th Assault Gun Brigade had also struck out for the bridge and had managed to stop Allied vehicles from using it. With shells falling so close to the crossing, immediate and decisive action was required if the threat was not to close the bridge more permanently. Luckily for the Allies, a well-aimed 57-mm anti-tank gun round destroyed one German tank and a bazooka halted another, and this disturbed the attacks enough to initiate a withdrawal.

This action, together with the many others like it all over 101st Airborne Division's sector, including attempts to cut the road at Veghel and St Oedenrode, stretched Taylor's resources to breaking point, but the arrival of his third lift in the midst of this fighting was a boon. The lift was not a complete success, however, for due to the thick fog over the English Channel nearly half of the gliders did not arrive. This meant that although a significant proportion of the division's 327th Glider Infantry landed safely, nearly half of their artillery pieces did not, and this was potentially crippling for Taylor as increased numbers of German tanks were homing in on the long and exposed Allied corridor. This vulnerable situation was exacerbated by the continued slow progress of the two British corps advancing on either flank. It might well be true that, like XXX Corps, XII and VIII Corps were not bold enough and that their commanders were too concerned about over-extending their forces, but it is also patently clear that these corps were given extremely difficult tasks to perform with enormously limited resources and poor opening positions. XII Corps, for example, had had only one narrow bridgehead over the Meuse-Escaut canal available to it before 17 September and VIII Corps had not been in a position to start moving its 3rd Division forward from the river Seine until the day before Market Garden began, and then did not cross the start line until the 19th. In such circumstances it is hardly surprising that the Germans on either side of the corridor had, resources permitting, the freedom to attack the Allies whenever and wherever they pleased.

The Allied situation was, therefore, far from rosy by the end of Tuesday 19 September. By this stage in the operation the flaws in the Market Garden plan, together with the frailties of airborne warfare, were being exploited by a well-motivated and flexible German army, which was still capable of landing hefty body-blows that sapped Allied energy and momentum. Operation Market Garden was in a critical state, and XXX Corps needed to pick up its speed markedly over the next few days if Montgomery's plan was not to die an ignominious death. The difficulty for Horrocks's men, however, was that just like the soldiers of 1st Airborne Division stranded in and around Arnhem, they too were vulnerable to factors over which they had no control.

FOUR

20–21 SEPTEMBER –
THE RACE AGAINST TIME

As dawn broke in Arnhem on the morning of Wednesday 20 September, buildings were ablaze and others were smoking in the rain-sodden rubble at the north end of the road bridge. Frost's men, who had been fighting for over two days and were very close to exhausting everything that they required to continue their battle, sustained themselves with the hope that XXX Corps would soon be seen rolling across the bridge. The officers, running from position to position to check on and encourage their men did all that they could to ensure that the force's scant resources were equitably distributed, but this became increasingly difficult as the enemy pressed in. Nevertheless, during the morning, signals were improved and a connection was established with divisional headquarters. At first a link was completed using a civilian telephone, the lines of which had not been cut by the Germans, a little later radio contact was made. In the conversation that followed, it became clear that it was extremely unlikely that any unit from the rest of the airborne division would be able to break through to the bridge, but the gloom was somewhat lifted by the news that XXX Corps should reach the southern end of Arnhem bridge during the late afternoon. Whether this was meant to boost the morale of the men, or was information passed on in good faith is not known, but whatever the motivations for providing it, it was hopelessly optimistic, for at that time both ends of the Nijmegen bridges were in German hands.

John Frost bridge taken from a position which would have been on the western edge of the airborne perimeter. *(Author's Collection)*

During the day, the German pressure on the beleaguered airborne forces became unrelenting as the Bittrich's troops inched closer to success. Infantry and armoured attacks intensified during the afternoon in an attempt to finally recapture the northern end of the bridge and open it to traffic. The fighting was at close-quarters and British ammunition was extremely low, but seven German tanks were destroyed before the PIAT ammunition ran out completely. It was at this time that Lt John Grayburn, already wounded twice, led an attack against a party of the enemy, which had begun to set charges under the ramp leading to the main span of the bridge. Having successfully driven the Germans away, some sappers removed the charges. The Germans returned and replaced them, but then were swatted away again in another attack led by Grayburn in which he was killed. This young officer clearly understood that the

Germans wished to have the option of destroying the ramp if XXX Corps reached Arnhem before the British had been overwhelmed, and Grayburn, awarded a posthumous Victoria Cross for his courage, was remorseless in his attempts to ensure that the bridge remained intact for the British tanks. The same was true of his colleagues as the British airborne troops fought bravely from slit trenches dug into verges as their previous defences crumbled around them. It was in the cellars of these buildings, however, that the wounded were crowded, and with perhaps only 140 British troops still capable of fighting, the number of casualties was impossible for the medics to count, let alone treat, and they included Frost who had been wounded in both legs by a mortar round. In these trying circumstances Maj Freddie Gough took command, but by this stage in the battle, there was relatively little for him to do as the fighting had disintegrated into fragmented struggles for individual buildings and tenacity was required more by the remaining troops than orders. Nevertheless, Gough did make an important decision. He asked the Germans for a temporary ceasefire so that the most seriously wounded could be evacuated to safety – and they agreed. Thus, during a battle that revealed the barbaric nature of warfare, there was time for a civilised touch between two elite fighting units. The Germans helped to remove the casualties and were helpful and courteous and then the hell started all over again. By this stage it was just a matter of time before the remaining airborne troops were overrun, but they clung on to the hope that what division had told them was true and that XXX Corps would arrive at any moment. As darkness fell, however, about sixty men had become casualties and the British tanks still did not arrive.

Meanwhile, the remnants of the 4th Parachute Brigade moved into the Oosterbeek perimeter, having collected in a position to the south of the railway line during the night of the 19th/20th. Departing at 0615 hr, 10Para followed 156Para towards the Utrechtseweg, but it

This photograph was taken on the afternoon of 20 September just to the east of the Arnhem road bridge and shows Spr J. Dunney (in the background), Spr C. Grier (on the left) and L Cpl R. Robb. These men were from the 1st Parachute Squadron, Royal Engineers, and had just vacated the burning van Lunburgstirum school to become prisoners of war. (IWM HU.2131)

The site of 'the Hollow' where, on 20 September, a mixture of parachute regiment battalions, including a large contingent of 156th Battalion, fought against repeated German counter-attacks as they sought to break into the Oosterbeek perimeter. *(Author's Collection)*

was not long before they ran into some enemy opposition in the woods. Trying to outflank it, a number of casualties were taken as more German units were encountered and the group split in two. 10Para made some progress as they moved away, but 156Para and brigade headquarters were hit by both SP guns and tanks and were forced to halt. The action made casualties of all but one of Hackett's brigade staff, and both the commanding officer and second-in-command of 156Para were killed. Swift and bold action was required if the survivors were not to be surrounded and annihilated, so Hackett took a company of 156Para and ordered them to attack and clear a hollow alongside the Valkenberglaan. The attack was a success and was followed up by the rest of the battalion, the brigade

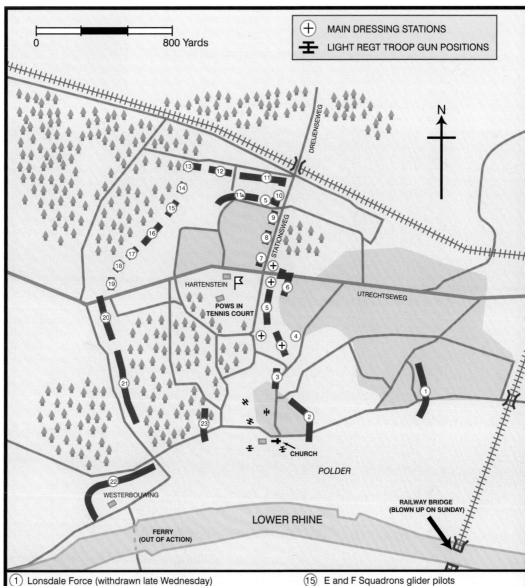

MAIN DRESSING STATIONS

LIGHT REGT TROOP GUN POSITIONS

N

DREIJENSEWEG

STATIONSWEG

UTRECHTSEWEG

HARTENSTEIN

POWS IN
TENNIS COURT

CHURCH

POLDER

WESTERBOUWING

RAILWAY BRIDGE
(BLOWN UP ON SUNDAY)

LOWER RHINE

FERRY
(OUT OF ACTION)

0   800 Yards

1. Lonsdale Force (withdrawn late Wednesday)
2. Thompson Force (becomes Lonsdale Force on Thursday)
3. G Squadron glider pilots
4. RASC (from early Friday)
5. No. 2 Platoon, Independent Company (from early Friday)
6. 10th Battalion (into reserve Thursday night, main road houses by Independent Company then)
7. D Squadron glider pilots reinforced by Independent Company on Thursday night
8. D Squadron glider pilots
9. 156 Battalion
10. Reconnaissance Squadron
11. KOSB (to 11ᴀ Thursday night)
12. and 14. Independent Company (until Thursday night)
13. Part 4th Para Squadron (into reserve Thursday night)
15. E and F Squadrons glider pilots
16. A Company, 1st Border
17. Part 4th Para Squadron
18. 9th Field Company
19. 261 Field Park Company
20. C Company, 1st Border
21. D Company, 1st Border
22. B Company, 1st Border (lost on Thursday)
23. Breeseforce (from Thursday)
Polish troops reinforced 7, 8, 20, 23 and other sectors

The Oosterbeek Perimeter.

Two army photographers eat a meal and are offered a cup of coffee by a local Dutch lady in Oosterbeek. The sign on the front of the jeep (partially obscured) says AFPU (Army Film and Photographic Unit). *(IWM BU.1150)*

The MDS crossroads looking east down the Utrechtseweg. *(Author's Collection)*

headquarters and few soldiers of the 10Para – in total no more than 150 men. Snipers caused some more British casualties, and then the Germans made repeated attacks in an attempt to dislodge Hackett and his company-sized group, but they were seen off. Here the British fought for the rest of the day, holding off the Germans and a few armoured vehicles, but doing little to improve their situation. Thus, at around 1700 hr and with only about ninety men left, Hackett led a charge out of the hollow which aimed to break into Urquhart's perimeter. Surprised and not a little scared by the sight of so many 'Red Devils' running screaming at them, the Germans froze and only a couple of parachutists were wounded as they reached the divisional area about 250 yards to the east of the Border Regiment. 10Para had reached the perimeter earlier that afternoon after a considerably less arduous journey, but they also had suffered more casualties and numbered just seventy men.

On Wednesday 20th the Oosterbeek perimeter, which had formed almost naturally around the Hartenstein over the previous day, saw a marked increase in German attacks as the enemy concentrated its forces on the area. Tanks, armoured cars, SP guns and infantry, armed with dreaded flamethrowers, all probed the perimeter at

This former hotel was a main dressing station at the MDS cross roads at the junction of the Utrechtseweg with Stationsweg. *(Author's Collection)*

various points during the day, and made assessments about British strength, noting any weak points. The British, meanwhile, were doing their best to ensure that an area with so little depth was adequately protected, and so as soon as 10 and 156Para arrived, they were quickly deployed in defensive positions. Both battalions were deployed in the north-eastern sector, 10Para where the perimeter crossed the Utrechtseweg and 156Para to their north beyond some glider pilots. Thompson Force were withdrawn to positions around Oosterbeek church that evening (and in so doing becoming part of a force commanded by Maj Dickie Lonsdale). At this time the perimeter was just over a mile long from its northern extremity, which was just south of the railway line, to its base on the river road. The width of the area was not uniform, it was just under 600 yd wide at its tip, broadening out a little to around half a mile at the Utrechtseweg and, with a little variation, remained about 800 yd wide until it got to the river where the Border Regiment, defending the high ground at Westerbouwing, added a little extra depth.

British casualties in the perimeter inevitably mounted on this day and were treated in two hotels, the Schoonoord and the Vreewijk, at a crossroads on the Utrechtseweg just to the east of the Hartenstein – a place that became known as MDS (Medical Dressing Station) Crossroads. It was to this relatively quiet area that the 181st Field Ambulance had arrived on Monday evening. With its surgical units working out of Model's former headquarters at the Hotel Tafelberg just to the south, its numbers were increased when the 133rd Field Ambulance that had arrived with the 4th Parachute Brigade, joined it on Tuesday. By the 20th, however, the MDS Crossroads was right in the front line, and as the fighting intensified some of the 400 casualties there, British and German, were wounded again. Indeed during the afternoon the Germans actually overran the area, and although the medics continued to receive patients, conditions quickly became barely tolerable. The 16th Field Ambulance,

Hitching a lift on the back of a Sherman tank, these infanteers from VIII Corps look ready to move into action. The man at the front is armed with a .303 Lee-Enfield rifle, the soldier on his left cradles a .303 Bren light machine gun, while to his right, the muzzle of a German MP−40 machine pistol can be seen. *(IWM B.10287)*

The Nijmegen road bridge taken from a position adjacent to the Belvedere looking north. *(Author's Collection)*

The Nijmegen railway bridge taken from the north of the Waal looking south-east towards the city. *(Author's Collection)*

meanwhile, was working out of the more serviceable St Elizabeth's hospital and had been since Sunday. The hospital fell to the Germans while 1st Parachute Brigade were trying to break through to the bridge, but British surgical teams continued their work and were joined by German doctors with whom they worked professionally, bonded by a common desire to save life. Other medical provisions were made more locally, such as in the home of Kate ter Horst by Oosterbeek church who did wonderful work assisting a medical officer of the Light Regiment, RA. These ad hoc arrangements very much reflected the way in which the British organised themselves in the perimeter during the 20th, making do with whatever was available and getting on with the job in hand, but as night came they were still desperate for reinforcements and above all wanted to hear that XXX Corps had reached the ever dwindling band of airborne troops at Arnhem bridge.

The memorial on the north bank of the Waal commemorating the assault crossing of the Waal by the 82nd Airborne Division on 20 September. *(Author's Collection)*

For the 101st Airborne Division, Wednesday 20th was not a bad day, for although the Germans still pressed them at every opportunity, they held on to their positions. Early in the morning the 107th Panzer Brigade launched another attack towards the Son bridge having strengthened, reorganised and regained their confidence after their failure on the previous day. The push was successful in that it again halted movement of XXX Corps vehicles, but a battalion of the

506th and a squadron of the 15th/19th Hussars eventually pushed them back and the bridge was not seriously threatened. It was not only the Germans that took the initiative on this day, however, for the 101st also expanded their positions in attacks, such as at Veghel, which provided them with a useful defensive buffer zone around important, but vulnerable, bridges. These successes were important in keeping the morale of the 101st Airborne Division high and their offensive spirit undiminished, and both were crucial to them in their ongoing battles to keep the road open against the hit-and-run tactics which the Germans seemed to be increasingly employing.

As Taylor's men fought tirelessly during the 20th to protect the objectives that they had already taken during the first few days of the operation, the 82nd Airborne Division were fighting to attain the necessary crossings for XXX Corps to advance across the Waal. During the night of 19/20 September, detailed plans were made for the 504th's assault crossing of the river which was to begin at 1400 hr. In preparation for this, the Irish Guards and men of the 504th fought that morning to clear the south bank of the Waal up to the area of the crossing site about a mile to the west of the railway bridge. By noon the 504th were in position and ready to go, but they were still awaiting the arrival of their boats from XXX Corps. It was an anxious wait which played havoc with the nerves of the

A German Waffen-SS defender of Nijmegen bridge, probably from 10th SS Panzer Division, lies dead after the successful attack on 20 September by parachutists of the US 82nd Airborne Division and the British Grenadier Guards. The Allied fight for the bridge had been costly in terms of time and resources for as XXX Corps's tanks began to cross the Waal, the Germans were on the verge of overrunning the British defenders at Arnhem bridge. *(IWM EA.38567)*

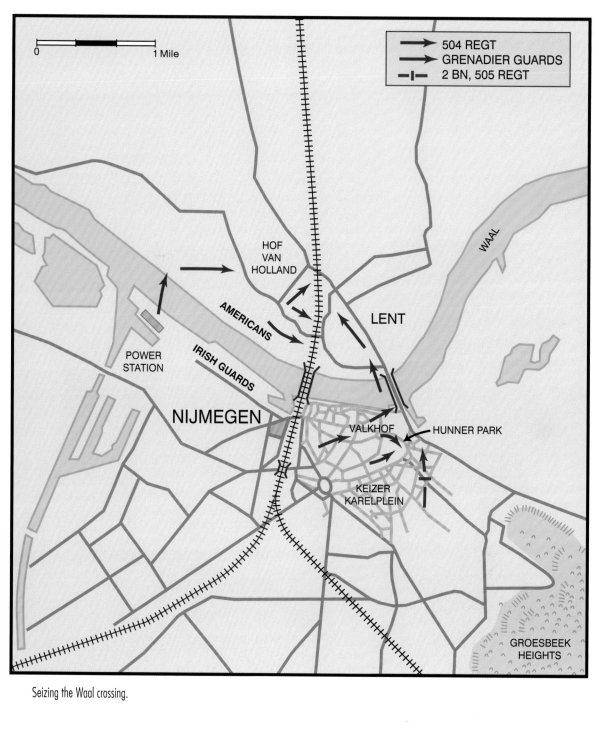

Seizing the Waal crossing.

The Belvedere at the southern end of Nimegen bridge looking north. *(Author's Collection)*

The Nijmegen railway bridge from the north side of the Waal looking south. *(Author's Collection)*

Hunner Park in Nijmegen. The southern end of the main road bridge over the Waal is just to the right of the park. *(Author's Collection)*

assaulting troops and did no favours to the men at Arnhem bridge who were expecting the Guards Armoured Division to link up with them at any moment. Indeed, the delay benefited nobody but the Germans, who used the time to concentrate additional forces in Nijmegen as the 82nd Airborne Division and the Guards once again attacked the southern ends of the two bridges, and, albeit slowly, made some headway.

The situation in Nijmegen was critical to the success of Market Garden, but Gavin could not forget that he had other problems to contend with elsewhere. With the fighting in the city making ever growing demands upon the division's resources, it was important that he received his rescheduled third lift and resupply drops. Unfortunately, however, the continued poor weather meant that the 325th Glider Infantry could not be flown in, only one company of 101st Parachute Artillery arrived and very few supplies reached their intended recipients. The manpower and resources situation took on great significance on the 20th, not just due to the fighting in Nijmegen, but also because five under-resourced parachute battalions defending a 12-mile sector of front were attacked that morning from the Reichswald. Co-ordinated and seeking to converge on Groesbeek, these attacks by II SS Parachute Corps in the area around Mook and Reithorst, and Corps Feldt around Wyler and Beek, posed significant threats to the crossing over the Maas-Waal canal and to Nijmegen itself. After a full day of fighting, the 505th managed to halt the Parachute Corps at Reithorst after withdrawing to some better defensive positions, but for a time the situation at Mook was tense after the Germans overran the Americans there and threatened the bridge at Heumen. Six British tanks from the Coldstream Guards Group managed to retrieve the situation with a counter-attack, but it had been a close-run thing. The battle against Corps Feldt further to the north was no

A German photograph of the northern end of Arnhem bridge taken after the surrender of the British airborne troops there on the morning of 21 September. On the left, the wreckage of numerous German vehicles can be seen. On the right are the remains of buildings which had been within Frost's defensive perimeter and the pill-box which caused 2Para so many problems as they tried to cross to the southern end of the bridge during the evening of 17 September. *(IWM HU.2127)*

less intense, indeed, both Wyler and Beek were taken by the Germans as the Americans gave ground in order to secure better defensive positions. Feldt might then have tried to exploit his success in the direction of Nijmegen, but whether it was a lack of boldness on the part of commanders or a lack of resources, the opportunity was not taken and the city was not threatened.

Back in Nijmegen, mid-afternoon, the final attacks were being put in towards the Waal as the American parachutists prepared for their assault crossing of the river. At 1430 hr the third battalion of the 504th Parachute Infantry Regiment, commanded by Maj Julian A. Cook, received the boats that they had been waiting for and began to assemble them. As they did so Allied aircraft bombed and strafed

The Union flag flying next to the Airborne Division flag at John Frost bridge with Arnhem, and the Dutch colours, in the background. *(Author's Collection)*

the opposite bank in preparation, while two squadrons of British tanks and approximately one hundred artillery pieces opened up with ten minutes of high explosives followed by five of phosphorous. Although a dense smoke screen was not achieved due to the strength of the wind, the Americans did not wait for more favourable conditions; at 1500 hr Cook's men took to the water in twenty-six dangerously overloaded canvas boats each containing three engineers. Battling against the Waal's eight-knot current, the men used their rifles as paddles to keep their boats on course, moving as quickly as possible across the 400-yd stretch of water. As the crossing began the Germans opened up with a barrage of fire that immediately sank a number of the frail nineteen-foot long craft. The British guns returned fire with high explosive rounds and the reserve battalion of the 504th did the same with their mortars, but the Germans knew that their lives depended on the Americans not setting foot on the north bank, so their fire hardly slackened. Approximately half of the boats made it safely across the river, and without a pause the engineers turned them round in order to pick up the rest of the battalion and then the follow-up force provided by the first battalion.

Cook's men, meanwhile, stormed across 500 yd of flat polder and an embankment that separated them from the enemy, and then engaged them at close quarters with bayonets and grenades. Few prisoners were taken as eleven of the assault craft returned with the next wave of parachutists. Thoughts then turned to the two bridges. Using fire and manoeuvre in small unit actions, the Americans made rapid progress towards their objectives, and by 1700 hr had secured the northern end of the railway bridge as their comrades continued their advance in an easterly direction. As these men approached the northern end of the road bridge, the Grenadier Guards and men of the 505th closed in on its southern end after a successful attack on the roundabout. Here, with many buildings on fire and the infantry doing all that they could to break through the German defences, including advances across the roof tops, a final charge took them up to the bridge itself. Without hesitation, despite the threat of the bridge being demolished as they advanced, the first four British

The centre of Valkenswaard, just a few miles south of Eindhoven, on 21 September, three days after the Irish Guards first entered the town. Two children chat to British soldiers in the foreground while other locals enjoy their liberation. *(IWM B.10148)*

tanks began to cross the Nijmegen road bridge, their guns and machine guns blazing – and the crossing remained intact. Why the Germans did not destroy the bridges remains something of a mystery. It is true that Model did not sanction the destruction of the bridge in time (his permission was not received until midnight), but Harmel did take a unilateral decision from his bunker in Lent to destroy the crossing, but although this was attempted, no explosion occurred. Whether this was due to human or mechanical error, the Dutch resistance having sabotaged the German charges or the fast work of sappers who immediately clambered over the bridge to disconnect any explosives that they found, is not known, but what is certain is that all four British tanks made it across safely just in time to link up with three privates from the 504th. It was 1910 hr on Wednesday 20 September and Nijmegen road bridge had, at last, fallen.

The German response, however, was immediate and sought to stop the Allies from developing a large bridgehead that could be used as a springboard for an advance on Arnhem. The difficulty for the Guards Armoured Division at this time was that they just did not have enough resources to exploit the confusion and disorder that their successful attack with the 82nd Airborne Division had created. Of the four Grenadier Guards tanks that had crossed the bridge, two were hit almost as soon as they reached the north bank by a pair of anti-tank guns, and although the two remaining tanks were joined by two companies of Irish Guards which quickly established a

11th Armoured Division of VIII Corps advancing on 22 September on XXX Corps's right flank. The vehicle on the right is a Sexton, a self-propelled gun version of the Canadian-built Ram medium tank. *(IWM B.10244)*

defensive perimeter, any forward momentum was immediately lost. Such actions show that the toll on the Guards Armoured Division as they advanced beyond the Waal was great, so great in fact that immediately after the Nijmegen bridge had fallen to the Allies, they were totally incapable of exploitation. At this time, of the division's three armoured groups, the Coldstream Guards were fighting on the Groesbeek Heights in support of the 82nd Airborne Division and the remaining two, the Grenadiers and the Irish Guards, were both still mopping up Germans in Nijmegen and in desperate need of a breathing space in which to reorganise, refuel and rearm. Meanwhile, spread out behind them and some 1,000 vehicles of their division was the rest of XXX Corps in a vulnerable 60-mile, 23,000 vehicle traffic jam – hardly the configuration for a rapid advance. As a consequence, just when more infantry were required it was almost impossible to get them where they were needed quickly enough. XXX Corps's 43rd Division, for example, had only just begun to cross the Meuse-Escaut canal on the morning of the 20th when they were ordered to Nijmegen. From that point on they had to struggle up the clogged road, were delayed by the Germans attacks at Son and by the afternoon, as the final attacks were being put in on Nijmegen, its leading brigade was just south of Grave bridge where it halted for the night.

The inability of the Guards Armoured Division to continue its advance towards the Lower Rhine that night did, of course, advantage the Germans who used the time to complete their withdrawal, reorganise and construct strong defensive positions on the road to Arnhem around Elst. Horrocks, meanwhile, ruminated on the fact that although his men were just 11 miles from Arnhem, his corps had effectively reached its culminating point and there was little likelihood of them linking up with the dwindling band of airborne forces at the bridge before they were overrun.

As a consequence of XXX Corps's inability to muster the forces necessary for an all-out attack towards Arnhem, it was just the Household Cavalry that pushed forward to test the German defences at Elst on the morning of 21 September. This probe, however, made no headway, and before long information was being returned to the leading commanders that the final few miles up to Arnhem bridge were going to be as difficult to cover as any other stretch of the road thus far. Meanwhile, as the Guards Armoured Division decided how they were going to tackle this problem, the airborne soldiers at Arnhem bridge were making their last stand. After a night in which their positions had been fatally undermined by further enemy infiltrations and the last seventy men were down to their last few rounds of ammunition, at 0900 hr that Thursday the battle at the bridge came to an end. The final transmission by the radio operator ended with the words, 'God Save The King'. Frost's men, amounting to no more than a battalion in numbers, had held the north end of the crossing for three days and four nights against sustained attack.

Two hours later, the Irish Guards received their orders to break through to the bridge, but it was not until the early afternoon that they were actually capable of setting off. Three squadrons of Irish Guards moved forward in single file up the main road with their infantry battalion, by that time reduced to just five platoons, sitting on the tanks of the rear two squadrons. They advanced into an area where the terrain was even less conducive to armoured attacks than it had been further to the south. The area between Nijmegen and Arnhem, or 'the Island' as it was known locally, was a nightmare for the Guards Armoured Division as it was often waterlogged, contained large numbers of drainage ditches, had very narrow roads and weak bridges, a raised main road and plenty of copses and farms for defenders to hide themselves in. After just twenty minutes, the Guards ran into a forward German defensive screen, composed of two infantry battalions with eleven tanks, two batteries of 88-mm guns, twenty 20-mm anti-aircraft guns and some of the survivors from the Nijmegen fighting – all under Bittrich's command. The unseen guns opened up and knocked out the leading three tanks very quickly. The infantry dismounted and deployed in the polder on either side of the road, and themselves came under German small arms, artillery and mortar fire. The Irish Guards at this point would have gratefully appreciated the support of aircraft, but none came to their aid. In fact during Operation Market Garden the Allies hardly used their air superiority for ground support, even though ever since

Men of the Airborne Royal Army Service Corps take a rest on 21 September having enjoyed a mouthful or two of a local beer. *(IWM B.10158)*

D-Day aircraft had played such an important role in the advance. Whether in a close support role suppressing and destroying the enemy, or an interdiction role in which the enemy were robbed of their freedom of movement on the battlefield, aircraft could give ground troops, and especially isolated, lightly armed and vulnerable airborne troops, welcome extra firepower.

The reasons why Allied air power was not inflicted more frequently on the Germans during the operation can be found in the complexities of airborne warfare. Early in the planning stages of Market Garden it was decided that air strikes would be prohibited in the area of operations during the lifts of airborne troops and their resupply due to the congested nature of the air space. With three lifts of troops, eventually spread out over five days due to the weather, and the subsequent resupply requirements of these men, the conditions over Holland were hardly conducive for Second Tactical Air Force to fly frequent support missions. Also, it did not help that when on the relatively few occasions close air support was available, poor communication between the ground and the air meant that it was not always possible to bring the aircraft down on to the required targets. This problem was caused by radio operators in the air support signals units on the ground not having the knowledge to get the best out of their equipment or the experience to understand complex tactical situations and the units with which they were working. The net result of all of this was that although the Allies had an increasingly strong grip on what flew in the skies over Europe, they were not in a position to exploit such strength.

Struggling for the rest of the day to make progress up towards Arnhem, it became clear to the Irish Guards that it would take some considerable time to reduce the German defences in the area. However, because British airborne forces no longer held the northern end of Arnhem bridge, XXX Corps began to think about the fastest way of linking up with Urquhart's defensive perimeter on the Lower Rhine. There were two ways of reaching the troops in Oosterbeek. One route, over Arnhem bridge was likely to take days to open up due to the Germans defences around Elst, but the other route, across the river, could be achieved by outflanking the enemy

A US 82nd Airborne Division soldier underneath a signpost to Nijmegen and Arnhem. With Mook only 1.9 kilometres away and Malden 2 kilometres away, it is highly probable that he is a member of the 505th Parachute Infantry Regiment and is standing in Molenhoek. *(ASOMF)*

to the west and moving up the narrow roads to the Lower Rhine's southern bank at Driel. The decision was therefore taken for the Guards to pin the Germans in their defences to the south of Arnhem, while other units headed for the river. These units included the 43rd Division of which the 130th Brigade had advanced from its overnight position at Grave and spent much of the 21st in a futile attempt to flush out non-existent Germans from Nijmegen. The push to Driel was to begin on the morning of the 22nd, but even this relatively limited advance caused XXX Corps difficulties, for by the evening of the 21st, just a single battalion of 130th Brigade were north of the Waal, while its sister brigade, the 214th, were 6 miles south of Nijmegen. Nevertheless, preparations were made for the attack, and a superficial link up between XXX Corps and the 1st Airborne Division was expected on the following day.

Although virtually no progress was made towards Arnhem on the 21st, the fact that both the 101st and the 82nd Airborne Divisions had relatively quiet days was a welcome boost to morale. During that Thursday, the exhausted American airborne troops could rest a little and generally take stock of their situation after up to five days in the field. The Germans had reduced some of their pressure on the corridor at this time because they too were tired and in need of reorganisation and resupply. The 59th Division which had been fighting at Best, for example, had run out of ammunition and had suffered prohibitive casualties over the previous couple of days. There was a small attack at Beek by the Germans, but this was deftly handled by the 508th and generally the day was calm for Taylor and Gavin. There was no such tranquillity for the British airborne division, however, which soon recognised that with the fighting in Arnhem at an end, the Germans were free to transfer the troops that had been fighting there into Oosterbeek.

The night of the 20th/21st was relatively quiet for Urquhart's men in the perimeter, a blessing that the commanders took full advantage of in their continued struggle to organise their defences and to gather and distribute the limited quantities of food, water and ammunition available to them. Hicks commanded approximately 3,000 officers and men in positions on the west side of the perimeter and Hackett a total of about 500 men in the remainder. At 0800 hr on the 21st, Harzer, who had been tasked with eliminating the troops at Oosterbeek, unleashed a number of heavy attacks at various points around the perimeter aiming for the Hartenstein. German superiority was already three to one and with reinforcements of men, tanks, guns and vehicles moving steadily into the area, that ratio steadily grew in the Germans' favour. As the day wore on and Harzer poured his fire into the pocket, its attackers began to call the area *Der Kessel* – the Cauldron. During that morning the Westerbouwing Heights were lost, a crucial piece of high ground overlooking the southern side of the Lower Rhine, the river itself and the perimeter. A counter-attack was arranged in the afternoon in an attempt to retake it, but the move failed despite inflicting heavy losses on the enemy. Had the Germans concentrated their resources at one point on the perimeter, especially against the weak spots that were inevitably opening up at various places, then, with overwhelming superiority of resources and the British lacking depth to their positions, they would have undoubtedly broken through. The fact that they did not, perhaps as a result of having too much respect for the airborne soldiers, a lack of boldness on the part of the German commanders, tactical inexperience or an unwillingness to take the heavier casualties that such a movement might incur, allowed the British to hold the area for a little longer. It was of course clear to Urquhart that in the attritional struggle that was developing in Oosterbeek, his men were at a distinct disadvantage, but he hoped that with the arrival of the Polish parachute battalions and XXX Corps (which he knew were near), his division could be reinforced or, in the worst case scenario, withdrawn.

The fighting in the perimeter became intense and, depending on German tactics, was at long range when the frightening six-barrelled Nebelwerfer mortar, artillery or SP guns were being used, or at close-quarters when the tanks and infantry attacked. Mortars and artillery rounds poured into the pocket and burst among the trees with deadly effect, while snipers plied their lonely trade and brought all movement in the open to a dead halt. The German prisoners held

A British paratrooper armed with an American M-1 carbine fighting from the ruins of a building in Oosterbeek. This was one of the first pictures received back in England from the photographers of the Army Film and Photographic Unit. *(IWM BU.1122)*

in the tennis courts of the Hartenstein were certainly not immune to the metal that was flying around in the vicinity and were given shovels with which to dig themselves in. It did not take long before buildings were in flames or in ruins and battle debris and bodies littered the landscape. The day was fraught, but the German attacks were contained, and like Frost's men before them, the British vacated the buildings, except for the wounded, and fought from slit trenches in gardens, fields and verges. There were many acts of collective and individual bravery at this time with officers taking their lives in their hands by dashing from position to position to visit their men, encourage them and give them orders. It was on this day that Lt Col Ken Smyth, the commanding officer of 10Para, was killed and Maj Robert Cain of the South Staffords, fighting just to the north of Oosterbeek church, was involved in an action that was to win him the only VC of the battle not to be awarded posthumously.

During this period, Urquhart was desperate for any information that might allow him to make plans for the battle based on fact rather than hope and supposition. It was with some relief, therefore, that he received a signal that afternoon informing him that 43rd Division was being directed towards the bank opposite the perimeter and would pass one battalion and ammunition over the Lower Rhine that night. Hopes were also raised by the news that XXX Corps was fighting near Elst and that the division's gunners had made contact with some Second Army guns near Nijmegen, and they had agreed to start providing the division with valuable fire support. This provision, supplied by the 4.5-in howitzers and 105-mm guns of the 64th Medium Regiment RA some 11 miles away, was remarkably accurate and with the shells bursting just yards from the British line, broke up numerous German attacks. The importance of this shelling was enormous, as it immediately discouraged and demoralised the attacking Germans, but if the airborne division was to be able to retaliate, it would require reinforcements and resupply. Urquhart was told that 43rd Division would begin to cross the river that night, but in the meantime the Polish Brigade was dropped to the south of the river near Driel.

German troops moving through Oosterbeek clearly wary of whatever was up ahead. The tentative approach of the Germans surprised many of the airborne soldiers in the perimeter which formed around the Hartenstein Hotel, for they believed that had the enemy concentrated their resources on a narrow front then they would have broken through their thinly stretched defences. *(IWM HU.2126)*

The Polish brigade commander, Sosabowski, was well know for his scepticism about Operation Market Garden and was not amused when his lift, due to arrive on Tuesday 19th, was postponed twice due to bad weather. While he waited with his troops in England to be transported into battle, he was given very little information about what the situation was like in Arnhem. His worst fears were confirmed, however, when he learned on the 19th that his gliders had landed in the middle of a fierce battle and then, on the morning of the 20th, that his DZ and mission and been changed. Even on the 21st, Sosabowski's patience was tested for one last time when his drop was postponed from noon to 1600 hr due to bad weather.

XXX Corps's infantry march up 'Club Route' behind the Guards Armoured Division. The gun on the left is a German 88-mm that was a superb weapon in either the anti-tank or anti-aircraft role. It had a maximum effective altitude range of 14,680 metres and a maximum effective horizontal range of 10,600 metres. *(IWM B.9982)*

The journey to Holland, once the Poles were eventually airborne, was not without incident either, for German fighter aircraft and flak were constant threats on the flight. Nevertheless, although there were relatively few casualties as a result of these encumbrances, the equivalent of one whole battalion did not arrive as forty-one aircraft had to return to England due to bad weather. A hail of fire from the Westerbouwing Heights, so recently taken by the Germans, greeted the 750 that did land, including Sosabowski. As if this situation was not bad enough, the Poles were unable to contact the 1st Airborne Division headquarters by radio and, although reassured that morning that the Driel ferry was working, it was found to be unusable. Contact was eventually made with Urquhart after Sosabowski's liaison officer, who had landed on the 17th, swam the river to pass on much needed information. Having confirmed that the ferry had been lost and saying that the division would endeavour to find boats in the perimeter and get them to the Poles, he then swam back.

Urquhart continued to hope that evening that both the Poles and a battalion from the 43rd Division would reinforce him that night, but as the hours passed, he recognised that this would not happen. Unable to find any boats in Oosterbeek, the Poles were left stranded on the south bank of the Lower Rhine, and still moving forward from Nijmegen, the infantry promised from XXX Corps just did not turn up. The Polish landings that afternoon did, however, have a positive effect on the battle for the Oosterbeek perimeter for the Allies. The appearance of airborne troops south of the Lower Rhine was of great concern to the Germans who thought that the force might well be used to turn the German flank and allow the Guards to break through to the Arnhem bridge. With this threat in mind, therefore, Bittrich despatched the 506th Tank Battalion with their sixty *Koenigstigers*, together with some Panther tanks and infantry, to attack off the main Arnhem-Elst-Nijmegen road in an attempt to destroy, or at least contain, Sosabowski's men. The attack was timetabled for the following morning, the 22nd, but just as XXX Corps had found, the terrain over which they were ordered to attack was not ideal for heavy armour.

Unfortunately, 21 September was not a day that moved Operation Market Garden in any meaningful way closer to success. Although there was relatively little pressure on the corridor during this time, the Irish Guards were thwarted in their attempt to break through to the Lower Rhine at Elst and a weakened Polish Brigade had arrived but then found that there was no way of getting them into the 1st Airborne Division's increasingly dangerous perimeter. The Allied offensive was running out of steam and as a result, Urquhart's men were fighting for their survival and quickly running out of time.

FIVE

22–26 September – Closing in on Oosterbeek and Evacuation

Before dawn on 22 September, two troops of the Household Cavalry, the reconnaissance assets of XXX Corps, set off down the minor roads to the west of the main highway to Arnhem in an attempt to break through to Sosabowski's Polish Brigade. Using the early morning mist to mask their advance, they found their way through the narrow country lanes and eventually fetched up in Driel. Although the final link up between XXX Corps and the airborne divisions had been made, there was no fanfare, no self-congratulation, only concern on the part of the cavalry that the Germans were not following their armoured cars and a desire to help the Poles defend their exposed position. Urquhart, meanwhile, faced another day fending off German attacks in the Oosterbeek perimeter with no immediate possibility of either relief or reinforcement. In fact Urquhart was so concerned about his division's situation that he sent his chief of staff, Lt Col Charles Mackenzie, and his chief engineer, Lt Col Eddie Myers, across the Lower Rhine to help facilitate a Polish crossing attempt and to see Horrocks and Browning to impress upon them the severity of 1st British Airborne's predicament. The two officers crossed the river in a two-man rubber dingy in full sight of the Germans atop the Westerbouwing Heights, made it to the southern bank, and then ran as fast as they could across the flat flood plain and into the middle of a battle.

'The Island' between Nijmegen and Arnhem looking north towards the high ground of Arnhem in the distance. Driel is to the front and out of shot. Elst is to the right. *(Author's Collection)*

The Westerbouwing Heights from the south side of the Lower Rhine. *(Author's Collection)*

The Union flag flying atop the Westerbouwing Heights commemorating the actions of the Devonshire Regiment. *(Author's Collection)*

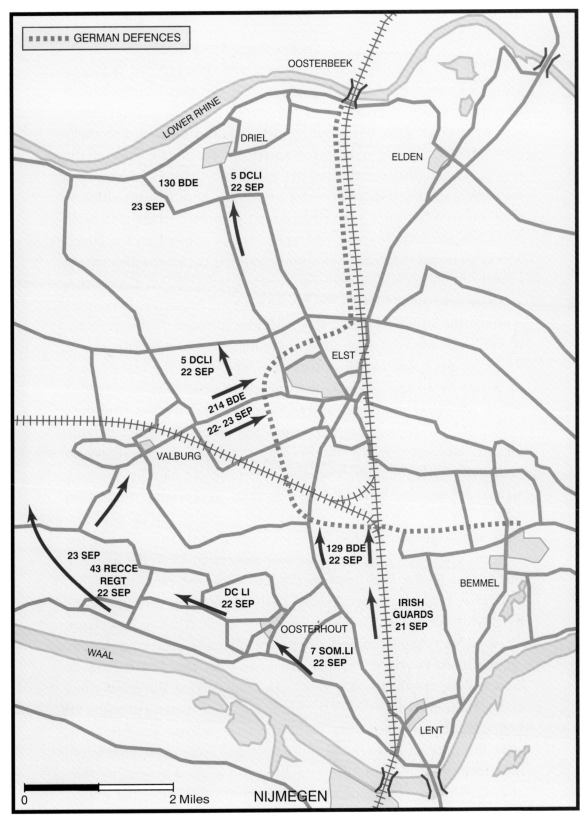

GERMAN DEFENCES

OOSTERBEEK

LOWER RHINE

DRIEL

ELDEN

130 BDE
23 SEP

5 DCLI
22 SEP

5 DCLI
22 SEP

214 BDE
22- 23 SEP

ELST

VALBURG

23 SEP
43 RECCE
REGT
22 SEP

129 BDE
22 SEP

DC LI
22 SEP

BEMMEL

OOSTERHOUT

IRISH
GUARDS
21 SEP

WAAL

7 SOM.LI
22 SEP

LENT

0   2 Miles

NIJMEGEN

North of the Waal — the Island.

Earlier that morning German armour and infantry had begun to advance from the Arnhem-Nijmegen road towards Driel. Initially the attacking troops probed forward cautiously in order to ascertain where the Poles were, but a full-blooded assault followed with shells descending on Sosabowski's positions from the north bank of the river and from Elst. For the inexperienced Poles, this German attack was a frightening experience and a number became casualties as their slit trenches were not deep enough to protect their occupants from the shelling. As the Germans slowly moved in on Driel, Mackenzie used the radio net in an armoured car of the Household Cavalry to communicate with the headquarters of XXX Corps and, as there was little chance of his getting to Nijmegen that day, outlined the situation of the 1st Airborne Division in Oosterbeek. Myers, meanwhile, endeavoured to organise a crossing of the Lower Rhine for the Poles, but he efforts were stymied by the chronic lack of boats. As all the airborne division could offer was four rubber boats, which, if used efficiently, could get perhaps two hundred Poles into the perimeter that night, the situation was far from perfect. Nevertheless, by the evening the 5th Battalion Duke of Cornwall's Light Infantry from the 214th Brigade of 43rd Division arrived at Driel and swelled the forces there appreciably. With them was a squadron of 4th/7th Dragoon Guards' tanks and two DUKWs, large amphibious vehicles stuffed with supplies for the airborne division. This delivery of men and resources to the banks of the Lower Rhine had been at the insistence of Horrocks who, somewhat belatedly, ordered 43rd Division to break through to the river with the orders 'to take all risks to effect relief today'. Thus, while 129th Brigade put pressure on the Germans attacking directly up the main route to Arnhem towards Elst, the 214th Brigade launched an attack towards Driel. Although taking the same route as the Household Cavalry that morning, the 7th Battalion Somerset Light Infantry attacked after the element of surprise had been lost, were not covered by early morning mist and were a far larger, and therefore more identifiable, attacking force. As a result, as they approached the village of Oosterhout that afternoon, the enemy opened up with small arms and anti-tank weapons and forced the

Two American soldiers on Nijmegen bridge watch tanks of the Guards Armoured Division moving north on 22 September. German barbed wire can be seen in the foreground together with a British sign directing the division towards the enemy. *(IWM B.10172)*

battalion to halt. Attempts were made to outflank the German positions, but the tight terrain made it very difficult to manoeuvre and it was some time before a frontal assault was attempted. Nevertheless, supported by medium and heavy artillery, the Somersets advanced stoically and took the village at 1630 hr. To exploit this success, and to add some impetus to the flagging attack, the Duke of Cornwall's Light Infantry pressed on through to Driel with its leading companies mounted on the tanks of the 4th/7th Dragoon Guards and their own armoured personnel carriers. Mackenzie welcomed these extra resources, but they still had to be

Brig Gen Anthony C. McAuliffe, the US 101st Airborne Division's artillery commander. His work on 22 September to thwart German attempts to seize Veghel was extremely important, and it was lucky for the Allies that he happened to be in the area reconnoitring a new location for his divisional HQ when the Germans attacked. *(IWM EA.49052)*

got across the river before the airborne division could make use of them, and that was easier said than done. The crossing of the Lower Rhine on the night of the 22nd/23rd, despite the preparation that had been put into it and the eager anticipation of Urquhart and his headquarters staff, was not a great success. A number of parachute engineers had crossed from the perimeter in order to help orchestrate the crossing, but even though the Germans were relatively quiet, by dawn on the 23rd, just fifty Poles had managed to cross in the few rubber dinghies available (and were immediately sent to reinforce the perimeter). The DUKWs, meanwhile, full of vital supplies but extremely heavy and difficult to manoeuvre, found it difficult to find an appropriate crossing point due to the saturated state of the ground and eventually slipped off a road approaching the river bank and ditched.

As XXX Corps linked up with the Poles at Driel, Germans further to the south, somewhat recuperated after their sojourn from offensive action on the previous day, launched a series of aggressive attacks on the corridor and the troops protecting it. Concentrating on Uden and Veghel in the 101st Airborne Division's sector, the Germans had deftly chosen an area that was not strongly held, but if taken would cause enormous disruption to the Allied convoy. The attack was conducted by the First Parachute Army's Kampfgruppe Huber in the

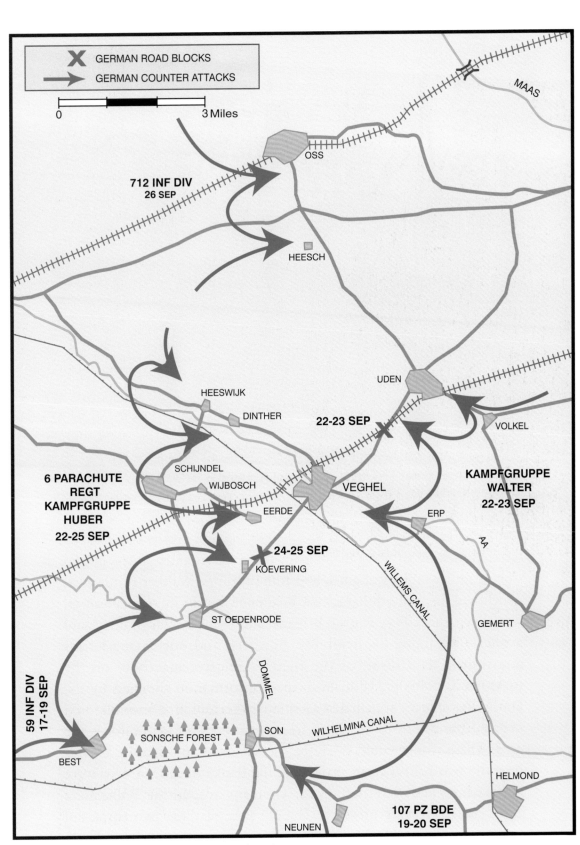

German counter-attacks against 101st Airborne Division and XXX Corps.

A Sherman tank passes the burnt-out wreck of a German Panzer IV near Uden on 23 September. The German attempts to cut the road to Nijmegen caused US 101st Airborne Division all sorts of problems, and they were desperate for armoured support from XXX Corps. *(IWM B.10375)*

west, consisting of a regiment from the 59th Infantry Division and some Panther tanks and guns, and Kampfgruppe Walther to the east, which had lost the 6th Parachute Regiment, but in its reorganisation was given the 107th Panzer Brigade and some extra infantry and artillery. Retaining his flexibility, however, and not having let his guard drop as a result of the enemy's relative inactivity on the previous day, Taylor, with the help of information supplied by the Dutch Resistance, anticipated German intentions that morning and ordered the 506th to redeploy from Son to Uden to reinforce the area. These troops could safely be moved from Son because by this time the two British corps protecting the flanks of XXX Corps were approaching and were putting the Germans around the Wilhelmina canal under growing pressure. The advance of these two corps did not, however, preclude offensive German action further up the corridor, and just as the advance party of 150 men from the 506th reached Uden at 1100 hr, Kampfgruppe Walther struck towards them. Outnumbered and outgunned, the American paratroopers did what they could to slow the German advance into Uden, but found it increasingly difficult to resist.

Meanwhile, at noon, Walther launched his attack on Veghel. More powerful than the push on Uden, a battalion of the 501st did manage to repel its first advances, but could not stop the enemy's tanks from then swinging in from the north and cutting the road. With XXX Corps vehicles ablaze, two villages under intense pressure and the corridor severed, the situation was serious, but there was only a limited amount that the American airborne troops could do against sustained armoured attacks. The Germans continued to advance towards Veghel where the main body of the 506th had deployed after they had been stopped from advancing up to Uden by the German attacks. Here, together with some men from the 327th Glider Infantry who were following them, they were organised by Brig Gen Anthony C. McAuliffe, the division's artillery commander, who happened to be in Veghel at the time. Pushing down the main road, the Panther tanks were edging forward when the leading tank was hit by American anti-tank guns forcing those that followed to stand off. For a vital few minutes while the Germans assessed the situation, the American airborne forces reset their defences and prepared for the next attack which they again repelled.

The ability of Taylor's troops to maintain their positions was, however, more severely tested when Kampfgruppe Huber attacked the corridor at 1400 hr. Huber was meant to have attacked at the same time as Walther, but, crucially, two battalions of the 501st held them up as they approached Schijndel to the west of Veghel and so prevented a dangerous simultaneous offensive. Huber had hoped to seize the bridge over the Willems canal that afternoon, but as they approached it a squadron of British tanks and a company of the 506th halted them. Determined to stop the flow of traffic up the corridor, however, Huber then decided to cut the main road to the south of Veghel, but here he ran into two battalions of the 327th Glider Infantry Regiment. The 101st Airborne Division just about

Two XXX Corps soldiers crouch behind a knocked-out German Panzer IV in the vicinity of Veghel in US 101st Airborne Division's sector. The tank is armed with a 7.5 cm gun, had a crew of five and a maximum speed 23.6 mph. *(IWM B.10376)*

Polish parachutists dropping south of Nijmegen on 23 September. As they were unable to drop at their intended DZ near Arnhem due to intense enemy action, the last lift of the 1st Polish Parachute Brigade had to be dropped near Grave. *(ASOMF)*

held on that afternoon as the Germans searched for a weak point in their defences to exploit. Throughout the day Veghel was hammered by German artillery which led to a number of casualties, but by nightfall the village was still in American hands and the road south open. At Uden, however, the road to the north remained cut even though the Germans were kept out of the village itself. Once again XXX Corps traffic began to build up just when they needed momentum and crucial resources to break through to the Lower Rhine. It was therefore extremely lucky that the pressure on 82nd Airborne Division from the Reichswald subsided on the 22nd, for it allowed Horrocks to push the Grenadier and Coldstream Guards Groups back south to help the 101st Airborne Division to reopen the road the following day. The Guards approached Uden during the night of the 22nd/23rd and sought to take up the best positions to assist the American airborne troops. The Coldstream Guards advanced towards Volkel to the south-east of Uden and the Grenadier Guards pushed into Uden, found it clear of Germans and scouted south towards Veghel where they ran into the Germans blocking the road.

During the morning of the 23rd the Germans renewed their offensive on Veghel – but this time British armour was in the area to add mobile firepower. Revealing German resource difficulties during this period, the tired Huber had been replaced in the west during the night by the 6th Parachute Regiment, which itself was weary and disorganised having defended the Meuse-Escaut canal. With little time to prepare themselves for the attack, the German parachute regiment put in a weak thrust and it was lucky for them that XII Corps were still some distance away at Best. In the east, however, VIII Corps had crossed the Willems canal on the previous day and immediately threatened German operations conducted by Walther.

The Waal and the Nijmegen road bridge a few days after it had been seized by Allied forces from the Belvedere showing XXX Corps vehicles moving forward towards the battle that was raging on the road to Arnhem. *(IWM B.10176)*

British airborne troops prepare a meal in the Oosterbeek perimeter during a lull in the fighting. Resupply baskets can be seen around the trenches together with boxes of ammunition and other pieces of equipment. *(IWM BU.1114)*

The British threat, together with the presence of armour and the tiredness of his troops, led to a half-hearted offensive by Walther's that was considerably weaker than that of the 22nd. Both attacks could, therefore, be successfully repelled by the Americans that morning and by noon the Germans were withdrawing. At 1300 hr, seizing the opportunity presented to him by a dissipating enemy, McAuliffe sent two battalions of the 506th north to link up with the Grenadier Guards and reopen the road. The Coldstream Guards, meanwhile, seized the village of Volkel, incurring hefty casualties as they did so, and then consolidated the area. By the time they had done this, the men of the 506th and the Grenadiers had linked up and traffic began to flow on the main corridor again. The effort required to defend what the 101st Airborne Division called 'Hell's Highway' was immense, but by the end of the 23rd they had been successful. With the help of the two Guards Groups and the threat of VIII Corps in the east, the exhausted Germans had been forced back – for the time being. Resources depleted, the 101st Airborne Division was therefore delighted to receive their artillery and the balance of their 327th Glider Infantry on the 23rd, and Gavin his 325th Glider Infantry. Both American divisions had done remarkable jobs thus far in ensuring the passage of XXX Corps to the Lower Rhine; having arrived at the river it was the job of Horrocks's men to release their British airborne colleagues.

The failure of the Poles to reinforce the Oosterbeek perimeter in any great numbers during the night 22/23 September meant that Urquhart's resources were even further stretched on that Saturday as casualties mounted and ammunition dwindled. Unfortunately for the British, unlike its two American counterparts, the division received hardly any resupply on the 23rd, although the Polish troops that had to turn back during the third lift did, at last, land in Holland. The complicating factor was, however, that due to the situation at Driel, they had to be dropped south of Nijmegen and march forward to the Lower Rhine. Also in Nijmegen that Saturday were Mackenzie and Myers who had been driven to the city that morning by the Household Cavalry in order to see Horrocks and Browning personally. Mackenzie conducted his briefings but remained unimpressed by the responses that his information elicited. As he returned north, Mackenzie just could not comprehend why there was not more urgency at corps level and resigned himself to telling Urquhart that relief from the south was not at all likely. Nevertheless, Horrocks's chronic lack of consistency during this operation revealed itself again on that same day when 43rd Division launched compelling attacks which sought to crack open the German defences at Elst and reinforce Driel in preparation for a river crossing into the perimeter that night. Once again 129th Brigade attacked Elst directly along the main road while 214th Brigade struck the village from the west and 130th Brigade slipped down the side roads to the west to Driel. Covered by a mortar smoke screen, 130th Brigade

Urquhart standing defiantly outside his Hartenstein headquarters on 22 September in spite of the proximity of the enemy. The penant that flies at his left shoulder can now be found inside the Hartenstein which is now a superb museum dedicated to the Battle of Arnhem-Oosterbeek. *(IWM BU.1136)*

moved slowly forward, but quickly found that their DUKWs were extremely difficult to manoeuvre down the narrow roads and highly vulnerable to German tank and artillery fire emanating from Elst. Even so, progress was made and they eventually broke through to link up with the 5th Battalion Duke of Cornwall's Light Infantry from 214th Brigade that had reached Driel on the previous day.

For the men of the 1st Airborne Division any attempts to reinforce them could not come soon enough. On the 23rd German attacks on the perimeter were ferocious. Infiltrating through gaps that their constant application of pressure on the British positions had

The remains of British military vehicles in a woodland clearing inside the Oosterbeek perimeter on 24 September. The Germans pounded the small area held by the 1st British Airborne Division with mortar fire and shells that not only destroyed jeeps and trailers, but also tested the nerves of exhausted troops who by this stage of the battle were largely fighting from slit trenches. (IWM BU.1142)

inevitably opened up, the Germans overran certain airborne positions, only to be counter-attacked and pushed back themselves. This intense fighting could not be sustained indefinitely, however, and there were certain parts of the perimeter that looked vulnerable to a major German breakthrough. One such place was the tip of the perimeter on the eastern side where some glider pilots, the King's Own Scottish Borderers and a mixture of 156Para, the Reconnaissance Squadron and the 21st Independent Parachute Company fought. It was, perhaps, rather fortunate that the Germans chose to focus their attentions in this area rather than elsewhere, for at least these men could withdraw a short distance without too much harm being done to the security of the perimeter. Had the Germans, on the other hand, decided to force themselves down the river road, then they might well have been able to surround the division totally by denying them

A German officer questioning a British airborne soldier during the battle of Oosterbeek.
Apart from a few exceptional cases, British prisoners were well cared for by their enemy.
(IWM HU.2133)

access to the river. It was, however, in the more northerly area that the Germans continued to push and, during the evening of the 23rd Hackett was informed by some Germans who appeared under a Red Cross flag that unless the British defending the area of the MDS crossroads withdrew by 800 yd, the area would be heavily mortared. The area contained so many helpless wounded that Hackett agreed to move back – but only 100 yd.

Troops on the south bank of the Lower Rhine were, meanwhile, preparing a river crossing into the perimeter that night to reinforce Urquhart's men, but they were not impressed when the newly arrived 130th Brigade produced only twelve boats for the assault. The crossing, organised by Myers, went ahead in spite of the lack of boats, but its successful execution was not helped by illumination of the river provided by the burning buildings in Oosterbeek and German shelling and mortaring. As a result, only another 200 Poles managed to cross that night, but there was hope, for at dawn when the crossing was suspended, most of the boats had survived. In the confusion, however, those boats were left on the river bank during the day, and there they were smashed to pieces by enemy shells and mortars. On Sunday 24 September, the chances of reinforcing Urquhart's division were as Mackenzie had predicted, slim. Myers continued to hold out hope that XXX Corps would make one final effort to get 43rd Division across on the night of the 24th/25th, but without boats he could not see how this could happen. In the background, meanwhile, Browning received permission from the Second Army to withdraw the 1st Airborne Division across the Rhine if necessary.

As the operation reached its climax on the Lower Rhine, there was still considerable fighting further to the south. On this Sunday, for example, with the main road having been reopened for just one day after the German attacks around Uden and Veghel, it was blocked once again. The problem began when a battalion of the 501st met an attack by the 6th Parachute Regiment at Eerde that morning and were close to being overrun. Just in time another battalion arrived with a squadron of British tanks and successfully counter-attacked. The Germans did not give up, however, and Battalion Jungwirth attacked around the Allies southern flank and headed for Koevering to the south of Veghel. When the 502nd at St Oedenrode heard of this situation they quickly sent two companies up the road to defend Koevering, but even when they got to the village before the enemy, they could not stop the Germans from cutting the road just a little further to the north. Once again the little momentum that XXX Corps had managed to recover after the previous blockage was immediately removed from them. This episode shows how, even after a week of fighting, the Germans were capable of applying just a little pressure on the corridor and yet could achieve significant results.

As the 101st Airborne Division decided how they could reopen the road at Koevering, the battle at the northern end of the corridor continued. By this time half of the Guards Armoured Division was fighting on the eastern flank of the salient that had been created to the north of Nijmegen, while 129th Infantry Brigade continued to hammer away at the German defences in Elst, and 214th Infantry applied pressure from the west. As various battles raged all around them, Horrocks, Maj Gen Ivor Thomas, commander of 43rd Division, and Myers, among others, surveyed the scene from a church tower in Driel and discussed the possibilities for the evening's crossings. After much deliberation it was decided that one brigade would be sent across, but later this was revised down to just one battalion, the 4th Battalion Dorsetshire Regiment, due to a lack of boats. Ever since that meeting took place in Driel there has been considerable controversy as to whether Horrocks ever really intended to reinforce Urquhart that night. Horrocks maintained that that had been his intention and that he had even planned for more troops to cross the river further to the west if all went well that night. The commander of 214th Brigade, Brig Hubert Essame, has said, however, that Horrocks saw no military value in the perimeter by this stage in the battle and was only interested in a crossing as preparation for Urquhart's evacuation.

Sunday 24 September was relatively quiet by previous standards in the perimeter. German attacks continued, but they were not as strong as they had been and there was a notable lack of sustained offensive action. Perhaps this German sedation came about as a

result of their undoubted weariness, but it might also have had something to do with the morale-sapping accuracy of British guns which, by this time, were positioned on the south bank of the Lower Rhine. These guns, which slammed their shells into German positions, broke up many attacks and were supplemented by the rockets fired from the Typhoons of the Second Tactical Air Force. With better weather and only one small supply drop programmed for the day, close air support could, at last, make an appearance in the skies over Oosterbeek. With shells dropping all around them, the Germans sometimes resorted to calling out to the airborne troops that they were doomed, should think of their loved ones and surrender as soon as possible. In all probability these attempts at this rather tame form of psychological warfare failed and undoubtedly only succeeded in increasing the British determination to see the battle through to the bitter end. The inevitable result of the British tenacity was, however, increased casualties. Among them on this Sunday was Brig Hackett who was wounded for the second time, on this occasion in the leg and stomach. The conditions in which the wounded were being treated by this stage in the battle were so poor that Col Graeme Warrack, the division's senior medical officer, having consulted with Urquhart, sought to organise a cease-fire with the Germans during which the casualties could be evacuated. Having talked to a local German commander at the MDS crossroads, Warrack and Urquhart's Dutch liaison officer, Lt Cdr Arnoldus Wolters, were transported to St Elizabeth's hospital

A Nijmegen street on 24 September with men of the 43rd Division, commanded by Maj Gen Ivor Thomas, taking a rest. At this time, and during the previous couple of days, the division had been fighting on the road north of the Waal towards Arnhem and elements of it had managed to break through to the Lower Rhine at Driel. *(IWM B.10274)*

where they were met by a German doctor and Gen Bittrich. During a very civil meeting, in which sandwiches were produced for the British airborne officers, a cease-fire was agreed and the two men were invited to fill their pockets with morphia capsules. The cease-fire lasted for two hours and came into effect at 1500 hr. During that time approximately 500 casualties were removed from the

Men of VIII Corps on 24 September taking a meal break during their attempt to shore up XXX Corps's right flank. Their speedy progression was crucial as the Germans moved from the east to engage the Guards Armoured Division or cut the single road along which they were advancing. (IWM B.10286)

perimeter to the safety of St Elizabeth's hospital. With such heavy casualties being taken, ammunition scarce and Mackenzie informing him that massed reinforcement of the perimeter by XXX Corps was unlikely, Urquhart's mind increasingly pondered the prospects of the evacuation of his division across the Lower Rhine. The Battle of Oosterbeek had reached a critical stage and Urquhart was desperate

Men of the 327th Engineers, US 101st Airborne Division, advance through a Dutch village on 25 September 1944 — the day that the final preparations were made for the evacuation of the British 1st Airborne Division from the Oosterbeek perimeter. *(ASOMF)*

The memorial to the evacuation of the 1st Airborne Division on the south side of the Lower Rhine. The Arnhem railway bridge can be seen in the background. (*Author's Collection*)

for information upon which to base his plans for the following days. He did not to have to wait very long.

The impact of the Germans cutting the road around Veghel over the previous few days had a direct impact upon preparations for the crossing of the Lower Rhine during the night of 24/25 September. With XXX Corps traffic backed up for 60 miles at times, resources required at Driel got stuck even when the road was opened. As a result only one lorry of boats reached the Lower Rhine in time for the crossing that night and even they did not have any paddles. As a result, although both the Dorsets and the Poles were ready to make a crossing by dusk that evening, the Dorsets had no boats and the Poles had only enough for one battalion. In these circumstances a decision was quickly made that it would be the more experienced Dorsets that would undertake the crossing, but this, of course, meant that boats had to be transferred to them. The time that this transfer took to complete meant that the crossing did not begin until 0100 hr on Monday 25 September and left considerably less of the night for the battalion to complete the task than it would have liked. Even so, every British gun and mortar in the area supported the assault and Oosterbeek was soon illuminated as British shells crashed into the Germans on the north bank. The Germans, meanwhile, wary of any movements south of the Lower Rhine and certainly keen to stop any reinforcement, also let loose with their guns and laid down a wall of fire on the river. As the British boats paddled slowly across the water, German shells destroyed a number of them while others were swept down stream by the strong current –

The top of the Westerbouwing Heights is today home to a restaurant with splendid views over the Lower Rhine. On a clear day buildings on the Waal can be seen to the south. *(Author's Collection)*

including a boat containing Myers. Out of what had initially been planned as a division-sized crossing, approximately 315 men made it safely across and were then immediately engaged by Germans atop the steep Westerbouwing bluff who lobbed grenades down on them. Those that survived headed for the relative safety of the adjacent wood, and few managed to breakthrough to the perimeter to take up defensive positions. The crossing upon which Urquhart had pinned so much hope had been an unmitigated disaster.

During that same night, the Germans reinforced their positions near Koevering in an attempt to make their road block more permanent. The 506th, however, attacked them at 0830 on the morning of the 25th having rushed there from Uden and from St Oedenrode and were later joined by an infantry battalion from XXX Corps's 50th Division and another battalion from the 502nd. The battle here was bloody and no quarter was given. During the day the Germans were reinforced by men of the 6th Parachute Regiment and held firm despite suffering heavy casualties, but by the end of the day Anglo-American pressure, including broad attacks by 44th Royal Tank Regiment attacking from the north and a brigade from 7th Armoured Division moving up from the south, began to pay dividends and their enemy was surrounded on three sides. During the night of 25/26 September, the Germans sensibly withdrew from the position, having bravely held on to the road long enough to cause XXX Corps's extended lines of communication significant difficulties. Indeed, the corridor came under pressure at several points on the 25th, including the area where the Grenadier and Coldstream Guards Groups were still busy aiding American airborne units like an armoured fire-fighting force that moved to engage the enemy where and when called upon to do so. On this Monday a German attack from the direction of 's Hertogenbosch, 12 miles west of Uden, drew the attention of the Grenadier Guards who moved forward and successfully countered the threat. The Allies were able to contain the weakening German attacks on the corridor, but in reality this amounted to little more than desperately plugging the gaps that were opening up at various places in their defences. This situation could not continue for much longer, the troops and their vehicles were at the end of their endurance and they needed a rest.

Much the same could be said of the forces that Urquhart was commanding in the Oosterbeek perimeter. By the morning of the 25th the division's headquarters in the Hartenstein Hotel was receiving reports of renewed German attacks against a number of weak British positions. By this time, however, all that Urquhart needed to do was ensure that the perimeter held for another eighteen hours, for he had received word in a letter from Thomas, the commander of 43rd Division, handed to him by Myers, that his division was to be evacuated. The withdrawal was codenamed, ironically considering the situation, 'Operation Berlin'. Urquhart signalled Thomas that morning to confirm that the evacuation would take place that night and he then lost no time in devising a plan and briefing his officers. The Germans, meanwhile, somewhat belatedly attempted to drive a wedge between the British airborne troops and the river by attacking towards Oosterbeek church. They were stopped, however, in an action that was crucial to the prospects of the evacuation that night, by a few airborne soldiers and some 75-mm guns firing over open sights at a range of just 50 yards. In such circumstances, the evacuation could not take place soon enough. But before darkness fell, there was one final shock for the division when the Germans struck a heavy blow at the northern end of the perimeter. Advancing with tanks, SP guns, and infantry covered by artillery and mortar fire, the Germans slammed into the British who found, to their horror, that their flanks were not secure. Attempts to exploit this success took the Germans to within a couple of hundred yards of the Hartenstein, but the day was saved by the Royal Artillery's medium guns directed from the roof of a house in the perimeter. Firing at a range of 15,000 yards these guns did superb work with their accurate fire first breaking up the advance and then halting it completely. The fighting here was at extremely close quarters and confused, but despite their enormous quantitative superiority in virtually every area of weaponry, manpower and supplies, the Germans found it impossible to dislodge the airborne defenders.

Oosterbeek church from the south of the Lower Rhine from where the evacuation of the 1st Airborne Division took place. *(Author's Collection)*

As these battles were being fought, the finishing touches were being put to Operation Berlin on both sides of the river. Just outside Driel, Thomas arranged that all the firepower that he could muster would cover the evacuation and hoped that the Germans would think that it was covering fire for the insertion of more reinforcements into the perimeter. Also being prepared were the boats that were required to take the exhausted airborne troops to safety. Sixteen assault craft and twenty-one storm boats were divided between two crossing points which linked up with routes that led through the perimeter on the north side of the river. Urquhart based his withdrawal from the perimeter on what he had learned about the successful evacuation at Gallipoli during the First World War. With a great emphasis on secrecy, the plan was for troops to follow taped routes down to the riverside with their positions being gradually thinned so as not to alert the Germans. The enemy would be kept occupied once the able bodied and walking wounded had left their positions by a façade of resistance mounted by the more seriously wounded and the transmission of some false radio traffic. These men would eventually fall into enemy hands along with the chaplains and medical staff who had all decided to stay behind to tend to their needs.

The operation began at 2100 hr on the night 25/26 September and was helpfully masked by a very dark night and heavy rainfall. As the boats began to cross the river, the guns and machine guns of 43rd Division and the medium guns of XXX Corps all opened fire. As positions were evacuated, soldiers stood on the river bank patiently waiting until it was their turn to cross in one of the small boats crewed by sappers. The deception measures worked well for three hours and it was not until midnight that the Germans recognised what was actually happening. Throughout the night the Germans poured shells on to the river in an attempt to disrupt the crossings and managed to sink some boats and damage others. Nevertheless, the pace of the withdrawal did not slacken, and at 0230 hr on Tuesday 26 September the last airborne soldiers left their positions in the perimeter and made their way down to the water's edge. When they got there they were met by a rather worrying sight, a considerable queue of men which, by dawn, could be counted in their hundreds. To have continued the evacuation in daylight, however, would have been suicidal with the Germans enjoying such good observation over the river and the south bank. So, although it was painful, the decision was taken to abandon the crossings. Caught in the open, cold, tired and vulnerable, some of the men that had been waiting for their opportunity to escape from Oosterbeek became casualties as they decided what to do next. Some decided to swim the river and a number drowned in the attempt, others ran back to the cover offered by various buildings and woods, but the Germans captured most of them shortly afterwards.

Operation Market Garden had come to an end. XXX Corps had not managed to cross the Lower Rhine at Arnhem but, ironically, the survivors of 1st Airborne Division in their unscheduled evacuation had. As these men marched back to Nijmegen a few days later to be addressed by General Browning, many wondered what on earth had gone wrong.

SIX

CONCLUSION AND AFTERWORD

A total of 3,910 officers and men managed to reach the south bank of the Lower Rhine by the morning of 26 September. The overwhelming majority of these men had landed in the first two 1st Airborne Division lifts, but this figure includes 160 men of the Polish Brigade and 73 from the Dorsetshire Regiment. From the 11,920 men that were flown into the Battle for Arnhem, 1,485 were killed (or died of wounds later). Most of the 6,525 men that the Germans took prisoner both during the battle and in Oosterbeek after the evacuation were wounded. When they advanced into the former perimeter at first light on that Tuesday morning, the casualties were taken away in ambulances and trucks to an 'Airborne hospital' that had been established hastily in Apeldoorn by captured British medical staff. There were, however, still some British airborne soldiers hiding out in Oosterbeek and Arnhem once the battle was over. Perhaps a couple of hundred men in total evaded capture and tried to get back to friendly lines. Among these was Gerald Lathbury who recovered from his wounds well enough to walk out of the St Elizabeth's hospital during the evacuation of the perimeter and joined others sheltered by locals not far away. Hackett was also treated in St Elizabeth's, but having survived his brush with death, he posed as a corporal and was eventually spirited away by the Dutch Resistance and nursed back to health. Some of these men successfully escaped and returned to friendly forces, including Lathbury, others were captured and taken prisoner. Many local Dutch people took great risks when they hid soldiers from the Germans, for if caught, they would have been shot.

LIEUTENANT COLONEL
SIR WILLIAM RICHARD
DE B. DES VOEUX, BT.
GRENADIER GUARDS
20TH SEPTEMBER 1944 AGE 32

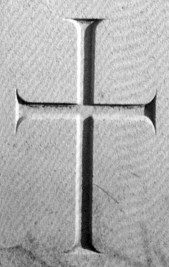

"ALTIORA IN VOTIS"
HIGHER THINGS
ARE AMONG OUR WISH

In the wake of Operation Market Garden the survivors of the three Allied airborne divisions involved had very different experiences. For the smashed British division the future was, for a time, in England where, by 30 September, they were reflecting on their experiences and recuperating after their ordeal. The Poles joined them, after a short stint in Nijmegen, in mid-October. The 82nd Airborne Division lost 1,432 men in the operation and the 101st a further 2,118. These casualties took the total loses for Browning's Airborne Corps to around 11,000, the equivalent of one full division. The American airborne divisions, in spite of their casualties, remained in Holland as a result of the Allies' chronic shortage of infantry. The problem for Montgomery and his Twenty-First Army Group was that a massive salient had been created in Holland and it took huge numbers of troops to hold it.

Opposite: The grave of the commander of 156Para who was killed during the withdrawal into the Oosterbeek perimeter on 20 September. *(Author's Collection)*

A peaceful scene at the Arnhem Oosterbeek War Cemetery. *(Author's Collection)*

The US 101st Airborne Division remained in Holland some considerable time after the end of Operation Market Garden. This photograph of the 'Screaming Eagles' was taken on 25 November 1944 as the division was being taken out of the line. *(ASOMF)*

James M GAVIN, Commanding General
US 82nd Airborne Division ALL AMERICAN

MISSION ACCOMPLISHED

After Action Report
MARKET Holland Operation SEP - NOV 1944

An 82nd Airborne Division memorial in Groesbeek. *(Author's Collection)*

The 82nd and 101st Airborne Divisions remained there in gruelling conditions until late November when they were finally taken out of the line. By that time both divisions had doubled the number of casualties that they had suffered during Market Garden. Of the three British corps that were involved in the operation, XXX Corps suffered 1,480 casualties and XII and VIII Corps, 3,784 between them. These large figures highlight the considerable fighting burden that the ground forces undertook during Market Garden, a burden that has often been overlooked because of the actions of the undeniably attractive airborne divisions (and particularly the British Airborne Division). It is also easy to forget the sacrifices made by the Dutch during September 1944 and immediately after. Beyond the risks taken by the Resistance and those that hid Allied soldiers, 450 men, women and children were killed as a result of the fighting in Arnhem–Oosterbeek, and many that were not permanently liberated became the victims of German retribution for the assistance that they provided to the Allies during the operation. The fighting, moreover, created 100,000 refugees in Holland and around 18,000 perished during the winter of 1944/45 when food became extremely scarce. Occupation had never been easy for the Dutch, but the last few months of the war were extremely painful with the Germans looting, destroying buildings and property and flooding the countryside, often with salt water, to slow the Allied advance. The Allied tide was, however, too powerful to hold back indefinitely, and when they swept forward again in the spring, the men of the 49th (West Riding) Division eventually entered Arnhem in April 1945.

But why had Operation Market Garden failed to liberate Arnhem in September 1944? The reasons are myriad, multi-layered and as complex as the operation itself. In the first place, the resources required to carry out the operation were enormous and Field Marshal Montgomery was never able to secure, to his satisfaction, everything that he required. The attack that was eventually unleashed was under-resourced in a number of important areas, the lack of transport aircraft and the weaknesses of the flanking corps were just two. These resource problems had a deadening effect on the operation, making the achievement of already difficult objectives that much more difficult. Thus, it could be argued that the tasks given to all three airborne divisions in Operation Market were too large, but planners were blind to this, partly because the airborne element was three times larger than for the abortive Operation Comet that sought to achieve very similar objectives. As a result, in spite of the 101st Airborne Division taking so many of their objectives quickly on 17 September, they could not prevent the Son bridge from being destroyed. Something similar could be said of the British Airborne Division not being able to take the Arnhem railway bridge on the same day and the 82nd Airborne Division being unable to seize the Nijmegen bridges before XXX Corps arrived. There would have been enormous positive implications for the Allies had these objectives been taken, as XXX Corps, on an incredibly tight schedule, would have been far better placed to build up the sort of speed and momentum that

A British soldier helping some aged refugees after Operation Market Garden in October 1944. After the Battle of Arnhem-Oosterbeek the Germans cleared the whole area of civilians with most fleeing north. However, all along the Market Garden corridor, Dutch people were made homeless by the fighting and many became refugees. *(IWM B.10523)*

they desperately lacked throughout the operation. As it was, the schedule broke down on the first day, revealing the massive over-optimism that the planners had in the ability of XXX Corps to advance quickly up a single road, cut in many places by water crossings, without adequate flanking cover and very limited close air support.

The ability of the airborne divisions to aid the advance of XXX Corps was greatly undermined by a poor air plan based on faulty air intelligence. The belief that prohibitive air losses would result if 1st Airborne Division were landed closer to Arnhem led to their

A meeting to discuss the forthcoming Rhine crossings, March 1945. From left to right: Maj Gen Matthew Ridgway, commanding US 101st Airborne Division; Lt Gen Sir Miles Dempsey, commanding British Second Army; Lt Gen W. Simpson, commanding US Ninth Army, and FM Sir Bernard Montgomery. *(IWM BU.2232)*

King George VI talking to officers of the US 82nd Airborne Division, near Nijmegen on 13 October. Partly obscured by the King is Gen Gavin, and to his right are Gen Andy March, commanding general of the US 82nd Airborne Division artillery; Col Roy E. Lindquist, 508th Parachute Infantry; Col Reuben Tucker, 504th Parachute Infantry; Col William E. Ekman, 505th Parachute Infantry, and Col Charles Billingslea, 325th Glider Infantry. Lt Gen Brian Horrocks, commander of XXX Corps, looks on. *(IWM B.10783)*

DZs and LZs being some considerable distance from their objectives. This gave the Germans valuable time in which to establish blocking positions in close terrain that was better suited to defence than attack. Airborne speed and surprise, a crucial weapon in an armoury that did not include heavy weapons or many vehicles, was fatally undermined. The air plan also demanded multiple lifts of the airborne divisions to Holland due to a lack of transportation aircraft, which diluted the initial attacking force available to seize objectives, giving bad weather an opportunity to intervene. Even so, the lifts should not have been spread out over the planned three days and a risk should have been taken to get two lifts into Holland on the first day. Had this happened then troops that had been required to defend the DZs and LZs for subsequent lifts could have been released to fight for crucial objectives such as Arnhem bridge or the crossings over the Waal. The benefit of hindsight, however, can lead to the over simplification of complex issues, and it should be remembered that Gen Williams, the man that took the decision to limit the lifts to one a day, did so for laudable reasons, but not ones necessarily conducive to the requirements of vulnerable airborne troops.

Airborne operations are fragile things, and if they are going to stand any chance of success, accurate intelligence is absolutely crucial. It is perhaps unsurprising, therefore, that out of all the weaknesses with the 1st Airborne Division's plan and all that went wrong during the Battle of Arnhem–Oosterbeek, it has been the intelligence factor that has so often been highlighted as central to Urquhart's difficulties north of the Lower Rhine. In fact, the accuracy of the intelligence supplied to the 1st Airborne Division was extremely good on the quantity of enemy troops and armour in and around Arnhem, but what it lacked at this level was any detail about the quality of those troops. Nonetheless, the planners of the operation were privy to such information and much more beside, and despite their greater knowledge of German de-ployments and strengths, they still thought the operation should go ahead. What was not given enough thought, however, was German reactive power and the flexibility that they might show in the face of such a threat. In short, although the Allies understood where the enemy was they were overconfident about their own chances of success based upon a low estimation of the enemy that they were facing. This was, of course, a mistake, for the Germans exploited the many weaknesses in the Market Garden plan to the full and revealed that a dangerous degree of complacency had crept into Allied planning in September 1944.

Many of the numerous flaws in the Market Garden plan became evident in the final few days before the operation began. However, with so many senior names closely associated with a plan that aimed to end the war in Europe by Christmas, there was little chance that the offensive would be stopped. The Allies hoped to catch the Germans in a disorganised state, speed was of the essence, there was no time to alter decisions once they had been made and Market Garden, therefore, very quickly attained an unstoppable momentum. This was not helped by Frederick Browning's desire to impress his superiors for his own ends and to take what was likely to be his final opportunity to lead his airborne corps into battle. As a result Browning did not question decisions nearly as much as he should have done during the planning phase and took up valuable transportation assets to lift his headquarters, which would have been far more useful in England, into Holland on the first day. Horrocks was another senior officer who failed to impress during the

Brig J.O.E. Vandeleur, commander of the Irish Guards Group during Operation Market Garden with the rank of lieutenant colonel, receives a bar to his DSO from FM Montgomery on 5 December 1944. *(IWM B.12493)*

battle. Perhaps due to his illness the commander of XXX Corps did not grip the battle as tightly as he usually did, was hesitant when boldness was required and was frustratingly inconsistent in his direction of the attack throughout. Nevertheless, it is quite clear that some of the criticisms that have been directed at XXX Corps over the years have been extremely unfair and have shown a lack of understanding about the difficult circumstances in which Horrocks was working and the limitations of armoured warfare. Just one of those limitations was the lack of close air support that was available to the advancing armour during the operation. The successful use of air assets and the gaining of air superiority had been central to the Allies' success in North-West Europe during the summer of 1944, and it was a massive blow for the Market Garden forces not to receive the sort of tactical assistance from the air that they might have expected. Close air support was provided to the airborne divisions for five days of the operation, but the number of missions flown during that period were relatively small: 97 sorties for the 82nd Airborne Division on the first Monday; 119 for the 101st Airborne Division on Friday; a few for the British Airborne Division on Saturday, 22 for the British again on Sunday and a further 81 for them on the last Monday. The paucity of air support to both XXX Corps and the airborne divisions was due to the fact that the aircraft of Second Tactical Air Force were prohibited from entering the airspace over the area of operations whenever there was an air lift or resupply mission. Perhaps if greater risks had been taken, close air support could have been provided more often with the beneficial effects of flexible firepower being enjoyed by both the lightly armed airborne troops and an armoured corps which was largely straight-jacketed by a single road. The fact that the air flank was not fully exploited by the Allies provided the Germans with a certain freedom of movement around the battlefield that they had not enjoyed for months.

When the 1st Airborne Division eventually received support from the air force the accuracy of the attacks was not perfect because of communication difficulties. Signals failure more generally, however, blighted Urquhart and his subordinates throughout the battle. All military units depend upon good communications in order to successfully accomplish their tasks, but with airborne forces the need for reliable signals is all the more important because of their isolation when dropped behind enemy lines. In the confused fighting in Arnhem and Oosterbeek, the fact that commanders could not communicate by radio forwards, rearwards or laterally, was a major disadvantage for those trying to direct the battle. The recognition of this problem by Urquhart had further serious implications for the battle, because it forced the divisional commander to try and assert his will on a developing situation using voice command, a method of command and control more redolent of battles in the mid-eighteenth than the mid-twentieth century. With Urquhart and Lathbury away from their headquarters at a vital phase of the battle, both men could only see the detail of a much larger picture. Shortly afterwards, of course, with Lathbury wounded and Urquhart trapped in an attic, neither men were in a position to see anything at all. In situations like this, the Germans were quick to exploit any weaknesses. As mention before, the Germans were not as badly organised or ineffective as the brains behind Market Garden seemed to think that they would be. A post-operation report by the 1st British Airborne Division remarked: 'It was thought the enemy must still be disorganised after his long and hasty retreat from south of the river Seine and that though there might be numerous small bodies of enemy in the area, he would not be capable of organised resistance to any great extent.' In fact, the Germans were quick to capitalise on Allied mistakes in Holland and to make the most out of any good fortune that came their way – and they were extremely fortunate. The fact that Model had his headquarters at Oosterbeek and had a chance to give orders to local commanders before he fled the area allowed the Germans to recover from the shock of the attack far more quickly than they would otherwise have done. They were also extremely fortunate to find an Allied document on a dead American officer which provided them with plenty of useful information that they could then use in the development of their counter-measures. However, it was the quality of the German commanders in the area that allowed them to exploit this good fortune so well. Outstanding general officers such as Student and Bittrich quickly saw what the Allies were trying to do, assessed their strengths and their weaknesses, and then acted. Men such as SS Captain Sepp Krafft, who immediately organised his men into a blocking position in Wolfheze to stop the advance of 1st Parachute Brigade on 17/18 September, were also important influences on the course of events. The inability of the Allies to pass XXX Corps over the Lower Rhine at Arnhem, therefore, had as much to do with some excellent work by the Germans as their own inherent foibles and failings.

Market Garden has gone down in history as a classic military failure, a grand plan drawn up by generals who then undermined its chances of success by their incompetence and buffoonery. In many ways the operation has come to be for many, the great Second World War example of 'lions led by donkeys'. However, just as the evidence for such a line of argument has been shown to be fatally flawed in the context of the First World War, with which it is most commonly associated, so it is of Market Garden. However, the reasons why Market Garden failed to achieve its objectives were complicated and cannot just be argued away by 'incompetence'. Indeed, not all would agree that the operation was a complete failure. The British Prime Minister, Sir Winston Churchill, wrote to FM Jan Smuts after Market Garden and concluded that he was glad the operation had gone ahead. 'The battle was a decided victory' he said, 'I have not been afflicted by any feeling of disappointment over this and am glad our commanders are capable of running this kind of risk.'

Churchill's belief that the Market Garden was a success requires qualification. The operation was a success in a way that it had not intended to be, it was an attritional success which, despite Montgomery's desire for a 'narrow fronted thrust', actually helped Eisenhower's 'broad front' to be successful. Although the Germans took heavy casualties during Market Garden, at least 3,300 men in and around Arnhem alone, it did not lead to the German army's immediate collapse, but it did play an important part in its eventual collapse. The loses imposed on the Germans, the ground and bridges that were taken were all, as Student later pointed out, crucial to the Allied victory in Europe in May 1945. But Market Garden was not as Montgomery argued, 90 per cent successful, as troops on the ground covered 90 per cent of the distance to the bridge at Arnhem. Operationally Market Garden was a failure as it did not fulfil its clearly stated objective of passing XXX Corps over the Lower Rhine. Nevertheless, Churchill was correct in his belief that the operation was, in September 1944, a risk worth

Dutch children lay flowers on the graves of the men of 1st Airborne Division in the Arnhem-Oosterbeek War Cemetery in September 1946 watched by local civilians and veterans of the battle. This touching and heart-felt tribute to those that fell continues to this day. *(IWM BU.10741)*

taking. *The British Official History of the Second World War* says, 'Operation MARKET-GARDEN accomplished much of what it had been designed to accomplish. Nevertheless, by the merciless logic of war, MARKET-GARDEN was a failure.' This is true, but one cannot help thinking that with just a little more luck, Market Garden could have been a success.

BIBLIOGRAPHY

PRIMARY SOURCES

WO 106/4410
WO 171/1256
WO 205/432
WO 205/433
WO 205/623

WO 205/693
AIR 37/1249
AIR 16/1026
WO 16/10–15
AIR 37/1214

SECONDARY SOURCES

Books

Eisenhower, Dwight D. *Crusade in Europe*, London, 1948

Montgomery, Field-Marshal, The Viscount Montgomery of Alamein, *The Memoirs*, London, 1958

De Guingand, Maj Gen Sir Francis, *Operation Victory*, London, 1947

Report by the Supreme Commander to the Combined Chiefs of Staff on the Operation in Europe of the Allied Expeditionary Force 6 June 1944–8 May 1945, London, 1946

Churchill, Winston S., *The Second World War, Vol. VI, Triumph and Tragedy*, London, 1951

Powell, Geoffrey, *The Devil's Birthday: The bridges to Arnhem*, London, 1984

Frost, Maj Gen John, *A Drop Too Many*, London, 1983

Hibbert, Christopher, *The Battle of Arnhem*, London, 1962

Ryan, Cornelius, *A bridge Too Far*, London, 1974

Angus, Tom, *Men at Arnhem*, London, 1976

Dixon, Norman F., *On the Psychology of Military Incompetence*, London, 1976

Hart, Stephen Ashley, *Montgomery and 'Colossal Cracks' – the 21st Army Group in Northwest Europe, 1944–5*, London, 2000

Rapport, L. and Northwood Jr, Arthur, *Rendezvous with Destiny – A History of the 101st Airborne Division*, USA, 1948

Essame, Maj Gen H., *The 43rd Wessex Division at War 1944–45*, London, 1952

Verney, Maj Gen G.L., The*e Guards Armoured Division – A Short History*, London, 1955

Rosse, Capt The Earl of, and Hill, Col E.R., *The Story of the Guards Armoured Division*, London, 1956

MacDonald, Charles B., *United States Army in World War II – The European Theater of Operations – The Siegfreid Line Campaign*, Washington D.C., 1963

Hackett, Gen Sir John, *I Was a Stranger*, London, 1978

Gavin, James M., *On to Berlin – Battles of an Airborne Commander 1943–46*, New York, 1978

Stopforth, R., *Arnhem after Arnhem*, Grimsby, 1992

Cholewczynski, George F., *Poles Apart – The Polish Airborne at the Battle of Arnhem*, London, 1993

Fairley, John, *Remember Arnhem*, Glasgow, 1978

Sims, James, *Arnhem Spearhead*, London, 1978

Urquhart, Maj Gen R.E., *Arnhem*, London, 1958

Hagen, Louis, *Arnhem Lift*, London, 1958

Deane-Drummond, A.J., *Arrows of Fortune*, London, 1992

Ellis, Maj L.F. with Warhurst, Lt Col A.E., *History of the Second World War – United Kingdom Military Series – Victory in the West – The Defeat of Germany*, London, 1968

Steer, Frank, *Arnhem the Flight to Sustain – The Untold Story of the Airborne Logisticians*, London, 2000

Middlebrook, Martin, *Arnhem 1944 – The Airborne Battle*, London, 1994

Kershaw, Robert J., *It Never Snows in September*, London, 1990

Baynes, John, *Urquhart of Arnhem*, London, 1993

Hamilton, Nigel, *Monty: the Field Marshal 1944–1976*, London, 1987

Green, Alan T., *The Border Regiment – Arnhem 1944*, London, 1991

Sosabowski, S., *Freely I Served*, London, 1960

Montgomery, B.L., *Memoirs*, London, 1958

Tugwell, Maurice, *Arnhem: a Case-Study*, London, 1975

Vandeleur, J.O.E., *A Soldier's Story*, London, 1951

Brereton, Lt Gen L.H., *The Brereton Diaries*, London, 1946

Horrocks, Lt Gen B., *Corps Commander*, London, 1977

Unpublished Articles

Badsey, Stephen, *Operation Market Garden and the Politics of the British Army*

Jary, Sidney, *Market Garden – A Revised Opinion*

Unpublished Diary

Wright, Lt Len, *Draft Account, 3rd Parachute Battalion, C Company*

INDEX